RESAMPLING:

The New Statistics

BY JULIAN L. SIMON

ISBN 0-534-21720-6

Resampling Stats, Inc.
612 N. Jackson St.
Arlington, VA 22201

TABLE OF CONTENTS

CHAPTER 8   The Statistics of Hypothesis-Testing
                     With Measured Data

CHAPTER 9   Correlation and Causation

APPENDIX 1   Sample Student-Teacher Discussion of
                     the Resampling Method

APPENDIX 2   Table of Random Numbers

PREFACE

This book describes a revolutionary approach to probability and statistics -- the routine use of Monte Carlo and resampling simulation to teach and do all problems in probability and probabilistic statistics.

The Monte Carlo method itself is not new. Around the end of World War II, a group of physicists at the Rand Corp began to use random-number simulations to study complex processes. By analogy to the gambling houses on the French Riviera, they called it "Monte Carlo." The application of Monte Carlo methods in teaching statistics is also not new - simulations have often been used to illustrate certain sampling distributions or concepts such as the central limit theorem. What is new and radical is the suggestion that Monte Carlo methods be used routinely as problem-solving tools in and of themselves for basic (not just complex) problems in probability and statistics.

Henceforth the related term <u>resampling</u> will be used throughout the text; it refers to the use of the given data or a data generating mechanism (such as a die) to produce new samples, the results of which can then be examined. The term <u>computer-intensive methods</u> is also used to refer to techniques such as these.

When I began teaching in the mid-1960s, I noticed that most graduate students, among them many who had had advanced courses in statistics, were unable to correctly apply the statistical methods they had studied. I sympathized with the students because I had had little training in statistics and none in probability. They and I could not intuitively understand the formal mathematical approach to the subject. Clearly, we needed a method free of the formulas that are nothing but misleading black magic to most students.

Beneath every formal statistical procedure there lies a physical process, and the resampling methods described in this book allow us to work directly with the underlying physical model by simulating it.

4

This insight is also the heart of what Bradley Efron felicitously labeled the "Bootstrap" (Efron, 1982).

The method was first tried with graduate students in 1966, and it worked exceedingly well for them. Next, with the blessing of the father of the "new math," Max Beberman, in 1967 I "taught" the method to a class of high school seniors. The word "taught" is in quotation marks because the pedagogical essence of the method is that the students discover the method for themselves with a minimum of explicit instruction from the teacher, rather than the method being taught as most subjects are, that is, handed down from instructor to the class.

After the first classes were a success and the results were published in 1969, three PhD experiments were conducted under Kenneth Travers' supervision, and they all showed overwhelming superiority for the resampling method (Simon, Atkinson, and Shevokas, 1976).

The method was first presented at some length in Part 4 of the 1969 edition of my book Basic Research Methods in Social Science. The most recent version is the third edition with Paul Burstein, 1985.

Before we go further, let's consider an example to make the discussion more concrete: What are the chances that three of a family's first four children will be girls? After various entertaining class suggestions about making four babies, or surveying families with four children, someone in the class always suggests flipping a coin. This leads to valuable student discussion about whether the probability of a girl is exactly half (there are about 106 males born for each 100 females), whether .5 is a satisfactory approximation, whether four coins flipped once give the same answer as one coin flipped four times, and so on. Soon the class decides to take actual samples of coin flips. And students see that this method quickly arrives at estimates that are accurate enough for most purposes. Discussion of what is "accurate enough" also comes up, and that discussion is valuable, too.

For some years, the method failed to ignite interest among statisticians. While many factors mitigate against adoption of new technology (including the accumulated intellectual and emotional

5

investment in existing methods), the lack of readily available computing power and tools was one obstacle. The advent of the personal computer has, of course, changed that.

Then, in the late 1970's Efron independently began to publish formal analyses of the Bootstrap - an important resampling application. Since then interest has exploded, in conjunction with the availability of easy, fast, and inexpensive computer simulations. The Bootstrap has been the most widely used, but across-the-board application of computer intensive methods now seems at hand.

"Basically, there is a computer-intensive alternative to just about every conventional parametric and nonparametric test. If the significance of a test statistic can be assessed using conventional techniques, then its significance can almost always be assessed using computer-intensive techniques. The reverse is not true, however." (Noreen, 1989).

It now seems appropriate to offer the resampling method as the technique of choice to beginning students as well as to advanced practitioners.

An early difficulty with the method had been that flipping coins and using a random-number table to simulate the resampling trials are laborious. Therefore, in 1973, with the programming assistance of Dan Weidenfeld, I developed the computer language called RESAMPLING STATS (earlier called SIMPLE STATS). Each command in the language executes an operation that simulates an operation that would otherwise be done by hand, working with cards or dice. For example, instead of flipping coins in the problem described above, we first give the command GENERATE 4 1,2 A, which tells the computer to chose four "1s" and "2s" randomly and store the result in location A. Then we command COUNT A =1 K, which tells the computer to go into A and count the number of "1s" (girls). Next we command REPEAT, which instructs the computer to perform (say) a hundred trials. And last, we command COUNT Z =3 J, which tells the computer to count the number of trials where the outcome is three girls. That's all it takes to obtain the answer we seek.

Though the term <u>computer-intensive methods</u> is now used to describe the techniques elaborated here, this book can be read either with or without the accompanying use of the computer. However, as a practical matter, users of these methods are unlikely to be content with physical simulations when a quick and simple computer alternative such as RESAMPLING STATS is available.

The final test of the resampling method is how well you, the reader, learn it and like it. But it may help you approach the scary subject of statistics with a good attitude if you know about the experiences of other students before you. Students as early as junior high school, taught by a variety of instructors and in other languages as well as English, have in the matter of six short hours learned how to handle problems that students taught conventionally do not learn until advanced university courses. And several controlled experimental studies show that students who learn this method are more likely to arrive at correct solutions on average than are students who are taught conventional methods.

Best of all, the experiments comparing the resampling method against conventional methods show that students enjoy learning statistics and probability this way, and they don't panic. This contrasts sharply with the less positive reactions of students learning by conventional methods, even when the teachers are the same people teaching both methods in the experiment.

A public offer: The intellectual history of probability and statistics began with gambling games and betting. Therefore, perhaps a lighthearted but very serious offer would not seem inappropriate here: I hereby publicly offer to stake $5,000 in a contest against any teacher of conventional statistics, with the winner to be decided by whose students get the larger number of both simple and complex numerical problems correct, when teaching similar groups of students for a limited number of class hours -- say, six or ten. And if I should win, as I am confident that I will, I will contribute the winnings to the effort to promulgate this teaching method. (Here it should be noted that I am far from being the world's best teacher, and I certainly am not among the more charming. It is the material that I have going for me, and not my personality or teaching skills.)

The RESAMPLING STATS computer program that handles problems incredibly faster than flipping coins, or using random number tables, is a simple language requiring absolutely no experience with computers. It does, however, provide a painless introduction to the power of computers. RESAMPLING STATS is available on both the Macintosh and the IBM personal computers.

The early chapters of the book contain considerable discussion of the resampling method, and of ways to teach it. This material is intended mainly for your instructor; because the method is new and revolutionary, many instructors appreciate this guidance. But this didactic material is also intended to help you, the student, get actively involved in the learning process rather than just sitting like a baby bird with your beak open waiting for the mother bird to drop morsels into your mouth. You may skip this didactic material, of course, and I hope that it does not get in your way. But all things considered, I decided it was better to include this material early on rather than to put it in the back or in a separate publication where it might be overlooked.

Now for a brief look ahead at the book. Chapters 1 and 2 introduce you to probability and statistics, and to the resampling method of estimating the probabilities of events. If you have studied statistics before, you can skip these chapters. Chapter 3 briefly discusses some of the basic concepts that statisticians use in their thinking. You might choose to move right on to the method itself starting in Chapter 4, and return later to read about these concepts after you have experienced them in practice. Chapters 5 and 6 get to work applying the resampling method to simple problems in estimating the probability of compound events, such as the chance of having three girls in four children. Chapter 6 begins the study of hypothesis-testing statistics, which continues in Chapters 7 and 8. Chapter 9 takes up correlation statistics.

So -- good luck. I hope that you enjoy the book and RESAMPLING STATS.

TECHNICAL NOTE TO THE PROFESSIONAL READER:

The material presented in this book fits together with the technical literature as follows: Though I had proceeded from first principles rather than from the literature, I have from the start cited work by J. H. Chung and D. A. S. Fraser (1958) and Meyer Dwass (1957). They suggested taking samples of permutations in a two-sample test as a way of extending the applicability of Fisher's randomization test. Resampling with replacement from a single sample to determine sample statistic variability was suggested by Simon (1969). Independent work by Efron (1977) explored the properties of this technique (Efron termed it the "Bootstrap") and lent it theoretical support. The notion of using these techniques routinely and in preference to conventional techniques based on Gaussian assumptions was suggested by Simon (1969). The bootstrap has been widely applied now for several years; other computer-intensive procedures had not achieved similar status as of 1990. Noreen (1989), however, suggests that that day is not far off.

ACKNOWLEDGMENTS

Many people have helped in the long evolution of this work. First, was the late Max Beberman, who in 1967 immediately recognized the potential of resampling statistics for high school students as well as for all others. Louis Guttman and Joseph Doob provided important encouragement about the theoretical and practical value of resampling statistics. Allen Holmes cooperated with me in teaching the first class at University High School in Urbana, Illinois. Kenneth Travers found and supervised several PhD students - David Atkinson and Carolyn Shevokas outstanding among them - who experimented with resampling statistics in high school and college classrooms and proved its effectiveness; Travers also carried the message to many secondary school teachers in person and in his texts. Terry Oswald worked day and night with great dedication on the program and on commercial details to start the marketing of RESAMPLING STATS. In 1973 Dan Weidenfeld efficiently wrote the first program for the mainframe (then called "Simple Stats"). Derek Kumar wrote the first interactive program for the Apple II. Chad McDaniel developed the IBM version, with touchup by Henry van Kuijk and Yoram Kochavi. Carlos Puig developed the powerful 1990 version of the program. William E. Kirwan, Robert Dorfman and Rudolf Lamone have provided their good offices for us to harness the resources of the University of Maryland and, in particular, the College of Business and Management. In mid-1989, Peter Bruce assumed the overall stewardship of RESAMPLING STATS, and has been proceeding with energy, good judgement and courage. He has contributed to this volume in many ways, always excellently. Thanks to all of you, and to others who should be added to the list.

CHAPTER 1

THE USES OF PROBABILITY AND STATISTICS

INTRODUCTION

WHAT PROBLEMS SHALL WE SOLVE?

PROBABILITIES AND DECISIONS

TYPES OF STATISTICS

LIMITATIONS OF PROBABILITY AND STATISTICS

BRIEF HISTORY OF STATISTICS

INTRODUCTION

If you already have some experience with probability and statistics, and want to find out about the resampling method, you might skip immediately to Chapter 4.

This chapter introduces you to probability and statistics. First come examples of the kinds of practical problems that this knowledge can solve for us. Next, it discusses the relationship of probabilities to decisions. Then comes a discussion of the two general types of statistics, descriptive and inferential. Then there is a discussion of the limitations of probability and statistics. And last is a brief history of statistics. Most important, the chapter describes the types of problems the book will tackle.

Because the term "statistic" often confuses or scares people, the chapter includes a short section on "Types of Statistics." Descriptive statistics are numbers that summarize the information contained in a group of data. Inferential statistics are estimates of the unknown, that is, they infer information based on whatever descriptive statistics are available.

At the foundation of sound decision-making lies the ability to make accurate estimates of the likelihood of future events. Probabilistic problems confront everyone -- from the business person considering plant expansion, to the scientist testing a new wonder drug, to the individual deciding whether to carry an umbrella to work.

To those interested only in learning resampling statistics, or who have some previous acquaintance with these matters, I suggest that you merely glance over this chapter and then proceed directly with Chapter 2.

WHAT KINDS OF PROBLEMS SHALL WE SOLVE?

These are some examples of the kinds of problems that we can solve with the methods described in this book:

1.   You are a doctor trying to develop a cure for cancer. Currently you are working on a medicine labeled CCC. You have data from patients to whom medicine CCC was given. You want to judge on the basis of those results whether CCC really cures cancer or whether it is no better than a sugar pill.

2.   You are the campaign manager for the Republicrat candidate for President of the United States. You have the results from a recent poll taken in New Hampshire. You want to know the chance that your candidate would win in New Hampshire if the election were held today.

3.   You are the manager and part owner of a small construction company. You own 20 earthmoving trucks. The chance that any one truck will break down on any given day is about 1 in 10. You want to know what the chance is that on a particular day - tomorrow - four or more of them will be out of action.

4.   A machine gauged to produce screws 1.000 inches long produces a batch on Tuesday that averaged 1.010 inches. Given the record of screws produced by this machine over the past month, we want to know whether something about the machine has changed, or whether this unusual batch has occurred just by chance.

The core of all these problems, and of the others that we will deal with in this book, is that you want to know the "chance" or "likelihood" or "probability" -- different words for the same idea - that some event will or will not happen, or that something is true or false. To put it another way, we want to answer questions about "What is the probability that...?", given the body of information that you have in hand.

The question "What is the probability that...?" is usually not the ultimate question that interests us at a given moment. Eventually, a person wants to use the estimated likelihood to help make a <u>decision</u> concerning some action one might take. These are the kinds of decisions, related to the questions about likelihood stated above, that ultimately we would like to make:

1.   Should doctors in practice prescribe medicine CCC for patients, or, should you continue to study CCC before releasing it for use? A related matter: should you and other research workers feel sufficiently encouraged by the results of medicine CCC so that you should continue research in this general direction rather than turning to some other promising line of research? These are just two of the possible decisions that might be influenced by the answer to the question about the likelihood that medicine CCC cures cancer.

2.   Should the Republicrat presidential candidate go to New Hampshire to campaign? If the poll tells you conclusively that he or she will not win in New Hampshire, you might decide that it is not worthwhile investing effort to campaign there. Similarly, if the poll tells you conclusively that he or she surely will win in New Hampshire, you probably would not want to campaign further there. But if the poll is not conclusive in one

direction or the other, you might choose to invest the effort to campaign in New Hampshire. Analysis of the chances of winning in New Hampshire based on the poll data can help you make this decision sensibly.

3.   Should your firm buy more trucks? Clearly the answer to this question is affected by the probability that a given number of your trucks will be out of action on a given day. But of course this estimated probability will be only one part of the decision.

4.   Should we adjust the screw-making machine after it produces the batch of screws averaging 1.010 inches? If its performance has not changed, and the unusual batch we observed was just the result of random variability, adjusting it could render it more likely to produce off-target screws in the future.

The kinds of questions to which we wish to find probabilistic and statistical answers may be found throughout the social and biological and physical sciences, in business, in politics, in engineering (concerning such spectacular projects as the flight to the moon), and in most other forms of human endeavor.

PROBABILITIES AND DECISIONS

There are two differences between questions about probabilities and the ultimate decision problems:

1.   Decision problems always involve evaluation of the consequences -- that is, taking into account the benefits and the costs of the consequences -- whereas pure questions about probabilities are estimated without evaluations of the consequences.

2.   Decision problems often involve a complex combination of sets of likelihoods and consequences, together with their evaluations. For example: In the case of the contractor's trucks, it is clear that there will be a monetary loss to the contractor if

she makes a commitment to have 16 trucks on a job tomorrow and then cannot produce that many trucks. Furthermore, the contractor must take into account the further consequence that there may be a loss of goodwill for the future if she fails to meet her obligations tomorrow - and then again there may not be any such loss; and if there is such loss of goodwill it might be a loss worth $10,000 or a loss worth $20,000 or a loss worth $30,000. Here the decision problem involves not only the probability that there will be fewer than 16 trucks tomorrow but also the immediate monetary loss and the subsequent possible losses of goodwill, and the valuation of all these consequences. The complexity of the contractor's decision problem may be seen in the schematic diagram called a "decision tree" shown in Figure 1-1.

3.   In the case of the decision concerning whether to do more research on medicine CCC: If you do decide to continue research on CCC, (a) you may, or (b) you may not, come up with an important general cure within, say, the next 3 years. If you do come up with such a general cure, of course it will have very great social benefits. Furthermore, (c) if you decide not to do further research on CCC now, you can direct your time and that of other people to research in other directions, with some likelihood that the other research will produce a less-general but nevertheless useful cure for some relatively infrequent forms of cancer. Those three possibilities have different social benefits. The likelihood that medicine CCC really has some curative effect on cancer, as judged by your prior research, obviously will influence your decision on whether or not to do more research on medicine CCC. But that judgment about the likelihood is only one part of the overall web of consequences and evaluations that must be taken into account when making your decision whether or not to do further research on medicine CCC. Again, the web of consequences and evaluations is sketched in the decision tree in Figure 1-1.

Figure 1-1
Decision Tree for Contractor Deciding
Whether to Buy More Trucks

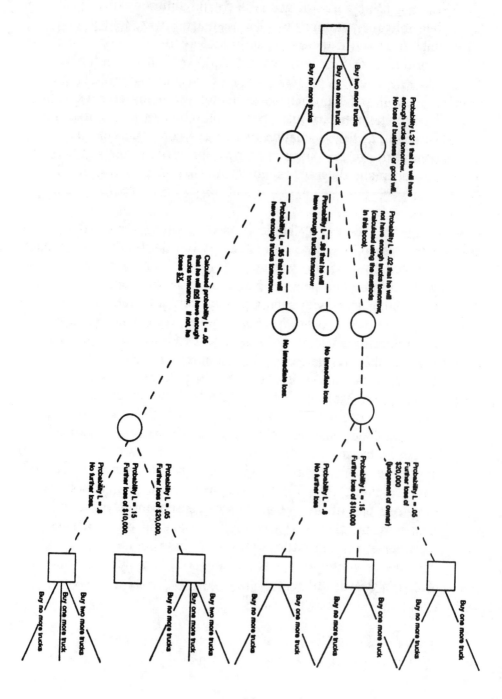

Why does this book limit itself to the specific probability questions when ultimately we are interested in decisions? First, simply, division of labor. The more general aspects of the decision-making process in the face of uncertainty are treated well in other books. This book's special contribution is its new approach to the crucial process of estimating the chances that an event will occur.

Second, the specific elements of the overall decision-making process taught in this book belong to the related subjects of "probability theory" and "inferential statistics." Though probabilistic and inferential-statistical theory ultimately is intended to be part of the general decision-making process, often only the estimation of likelihoods is done systematically, and the rest of the decision-making process -- for example, the decision whether or not to proceed with further research on medicine CCC -- is done in informal and unsystematic fashion. This is regrettable, but the fact that this is standard practice is an additional reason why the treatment of inferential statistics and probability in this book does not suffer from incompleteness.

A third reason that this book covers only inferential statistics and not decision statistics because most college and university statistics courses and books are limited to inferential statistics, especially those courses and books for students in the social sciences.

TYPES OF STATISTICS

The term *statistics* sometimes causes confusion and therefore needs explanation.

A statistic is a <u>number</u>. There are two kinds of statistics, summarization (descriptive) statistics and probability statistics. The most important summarization statistics are the total, averages such as the mean and median, the distribution, the range, and other measures of variation. Such statistics are nothing new to you; you have been using many of them all your life. Inferential statistics, which this book deals with, uses descriptive statistics as its input.

Inferential statistics can be used for two purposes: to aid scientific <u>understanding</u> by estimating the probability that a statement is

17

true or not, and to aid in making <u>sound decisions</u> by estimating which alternative among a range of possibilities is most desirable.

LIMITATIONS OF PROBABILITY AND STATISTICS

Statistical testing is not equivalent to social-science research, and research is not the same as statistical testing. Rather, statistical theory is a handmaiden of research, often but not always necessary in the research process.

A working knowledge of the basic ideas of statistics, especially the elements of probability, is unsurpassed in its general value to everyone in a modern society. Statistics and probability help clarify one's thinking and improve one's capacity to deal with practical problems and to understand the world. And to be efficient, a social scientist is almost sure to need statistics and probability.

On the other hand, important research has been done by people with absolutely no formal knowledge of statistics. And a little study of statistics sometimes befuddles students into thinking that statistical principles are guides to research design and analysis. This mistaken belief only inhibits the exercise of sound research thinking. Kinsey put it this way:

"However satisfactory the standard deviations may be, no statistical treatment can put validity into generalizations which are based on data that were not reasonably accurate and complete to begin with. It is unfortunate that academic departments so often offer courses on the statistical manipulation of human material to students who have little understanding of the problems involved in securing the original data. ... When training in these things replaces or at least precedes some of the college courses on the mathematical treatment of data, we shall come nearer to having a science of human behavior. (Kinsey et al., 1948, p. 35)."

In much - even most - research in social and physical sciences, statistical testing is not necessary. This is because where there are big differences between different sorts of circumstances -- for example, if one medicine cures 90 patients out of 100 and the other medicine cures only 10 patients out of 100 -- then we do not need refined statistical tests to tell us whether or not there really is a difference. And the best research is that which shows big differences, because it is the big differences that really matter. If the researcher finds that she/he must use refined statistical tests to reveal whether there are differences, the differences do not matter much.

To repeat then, most research does not need the kind of statistical manipulation that will be described in this book. But most decision problems do need the kind of probabilistic and statistical input that is described in this book.

Another matter: If the raw data are of poor quality, probabilistic and statistical manipulation cannot be very useful. In the example of the contractor and her trucks, if the contractor's estimate that a given truck has a 1 in 10 chance of being out-of-order on a given day is very inaccurate, then our calculation of the probability that four or more trucks will be out of order on a given day will not be helpful, and may be misleading. To put it another way, one cannot make bread without flour, yeast, and water. And good raw data are the flour, yeast and water necessary to get an accurate estimate of a probability. The most refined statistical and probabilistic manipulations are useless if the input data are bad. Therefore, we should constantly direct our attention to ensuring that the data upon which we base our calculations is good data.

BRIEF HISTORY OF STATISTICS

In ancient times, mathematics developed from the needs of governments and rich men to number armies, flocks, and especially to count the taxpayers and their possessions. Up until the beginning of the 20th century, the term *statistic* meant the number of something -- soldiers, births, or what-have-you. In many cases, the term *statistic* still means the number of something; the most important statistics for the United States are in the *Statistical Abstract of the United States*. As noted above, these numbers are what are now known as descriptive

19

statistics. This book will not deal at all with the making or interpretation of descriptive statistics, because the topic is handled very well in most conventional statistics texts.

Another stream of thought entered the field of probability and statistics by way of gambling in France in the 17th century. Throughout history people had learned about the odds in gambling games by trial-and-error experience. But in the year 1654, the French nobleman Chevalier de Mere asked the great mathematician and philosopher Pascal to help him figure out what the odds ought to be in some gambling games. Pascal, the famous Fermat, and others went on to develop modern probability theory.

Later on these two streams of thought came together. People wanted to know how accurate their descriptive statistics were -- not only the descriptive statistics originating from sample surveys, but also the numbers arising from experiments. Statisticians began to apply the theory of probability to the accuracy of the data arising from sample surveys and experiments, and that is the theory of *inferential statistics*.

Here we find a guidepost: probability theory is relevant whenever there is uncertainty about events occurring in the world, or in the numbers describing those events.

Later, probability theory began to be developed for another context in which there is uncertainty -- the context of decision-making. Descriptive statistics like those used by insurance companies -- for example, the number of people per thousand in each age bracket who die in a five-year period -- have for a long time been used in making decisions about how much to charge people for insurance policies. But in the modern probabilistic theory of decision-making in business, politics and war, the emphasis is different; in such situations the emphasis is on methods of <u>combining</u> estimates of probabilities that depend upon each other in complicated ways in order to arrive at the best decision. This is a return to the gambling-game origin of probability and statistics. In contrast, in most insurance situations the likelihoods can be estimated with rather good precision on the basis of a great many observations without complex calculation, and the main statistical task is gathering this information. In business and political

20

decision-making situations, however, one usually works with probabilities that are based on very limited information, often little better than guesses. And the job is how best to combine these guesses about various likelihoods into an overall likelihood estimate.

Estimating probabilities with conventional mathematical methods is often so complex that the process scares many people. And properly so, because its difficulty leads to errors. The statistics profession has expressed great concern about the widespread use of conventional tests whose foundations are poorly understood. The ready availability of statistical computer packages that can easily perform these tests with a single command, regardless of whether the user understands what is going on or whether the test is appropriate, has exacerbated this problem. This led John Tukey to turn the field toward descriptive statistics with his techniques of "exploratory data analysis" (Tukey, 1977). These methods are well described in many texts.

Probabilistic analysis also is crucial, however. Judgments about whether to allow a new medicine on the market, or whether to adjust the screw machine, require more than eyeballing data to assess chance variability. But until now, the teaching of probabilistic statistics, with its abstruse structure of mathematical formulas, tables of values, and restrictive assumptions concerning data distribution -- all of which separate the student from the actual data or physical process under consideration -- have been an insurmountable obstacle.

Now, however, the resampling method -- whose history was briefly told in the Introduction -- has come along to enable people to obtain the benefits of statistics and predictability without the shortcomings of conventional methods -- free of mathematical formulas and restrictive assumptions. Resampling's repeated trial and experimentation enable the data (or a data generating mechanism representing a hypothesis) to express its own properties. We hope you profit from it and enjoy it!

CHAPTER 2

THE RESAMPLING METHOD OF SOLVING PROBLEMS

INTRODUCTION

HOW RESAMPLING DIFFERS FROM THE CONVENTIONAL APPROACH

A NOTE TO THE TEACHER (AND STUDENT)

> **For Whom, When, is the Resampling Approach Good?**
>
> **Should the Resampling Approach be Taught by Itself, or Along with the Conventional Method?**
>
> **About Teaching Resampling**
>
> **Advantages and Disadvantges of the Resampling Method**

INTRODUCTION

This chapter discusses the resampling method of solving problems in probability and statistics, and how it differs from the conventional approach. A simple illustrative problem is posed, and then the step-by-step solution with resampling is shown, using both hand methods and the computer program RESAMPLING STATS. The older conventional approach to such a problem is then discussed. The conventional analytic method requires that you understand complex formulae, and too often one selects the wrong formula. In contrast, resampling requires that you understand the physical problem fully. Then you simulate a statistical model of the physical problem with techniques that are intuitively obvious, and you estimate the probability with repeated random sampling.

There follows an "Afternote to the Teacher," which may also interest some students. It discusses the advantages and disadvantages of resampling, and describes experimental evidence for its success in solving problems as well as in arousing and keeping the interest of students.

HOW RESAMPLING DIFFERS FROM THE CONVENTIONAL APPROACH

Recall the problem of the construction firm that owns 20 earthmoving trucks. The chance that any one truck will break down on any given day is about 1 in 10, based on past experience. You want to know the probability that on a particular day -- tomorrow -- four or more trucks will be out of action. The resampling approach produces the estimate as follows: We collect 10 coins, and mark one of them with a pen or pencil or tape as being the coin that represents "out-of-order;" the other nine coins stand for "in operation." This set of 10 coins is a "model" of a situation where there is a one-in-ten chance, or a probability of .10 (10 percent), of one particular truck being out-of-order on a given day. Next, we put the coins into a little jar or urn, draw out one coin, and mark down whether or not that coin is the coin marked "out-of-order". That drawing of the single coin from the urn represents the chance that any one given truck among our twenty trucks (perhaps the one with the lowest license-plate number) will be out-of-order tomorrow.

Then we put the drawn coin back in the urn, shake all the coins around, and again draw out a coin. We mark down whether that second-drawing coin is or is not the "out-of-order" coin, and that outcome stands for a second truck in the fleet. We do this twenty times to represent our twenty trucks, replacing the coin after each drawing, of course. Those twenty drawings represent one day.

At the end of the twenty draws we count how many out-of-orders we have gotten, checking whether there are four or more out-of-orders. If there are four or more, we write down in another column "yes"; if not, we write "no." The work we have done up to now represents one experimental trial of the model for a single day.

Then we repeat perhaps 50 or 100 times the entire experiment described above. Each of those 50 or 100 experimental trials represents a single day. When we have collected evidence for 50 or 100 experimental days, we determine the proportion of the experimental days on which four or more trucks are out of order. That proportion estimates for us the probability that four or more trucks will be out of order on a given day -- the answer we seek. This procedure is an example of the resampling method of statistical estimation.

A more direct way to answer this question would be to examine the firm's actual records for the past 100 days and 500 days to determine how many days four or more trucks were out of order. But the resampling procedure described above gives us an estimate even if we have no information about the number of days. It is frequently the case in the workaday world that we must make estimates on the basis of insufficient history about an event.

A quicker resampling method than the coins could be obtained with twenty ten-sided spinners. Each one of the spinners, marked with one of its ten sides as "out-of-order," would indicate the chance of a single truck being out of order on a given day. A single throw of the twenty spinners allows us to count whether four or more trucks turn up out of order. So in a single throw of the twenty spinners we can get an experimental trial that represents a single day. And in a hundred quick throws of the twenty spinners -- which probably takes less than 5 minutes -- we can get a fast and reasonably-accurate answer to our question. But obtaining ten-sided spinners might be a nuisance.

Another fast way that needs no special equipment is using a table of "random digits," such as is found in Appendix 2. If we say that the digit "zero" represents "out-of-order" and the digits "1-9" represent "in operation," then any one random digit gives us a trial observation for a single truck. To get an experimental trial for a single day we look at twenty digits and count the number of zeros. If the number of zeros is four or more, then we write "yes." We then look at one hundred or two hundred sets of twenty digits and count the proportion of sets whose twenty digits show four or more trucks being "out-of-order." Once again, that proportion estimates the probability that four or more trucks will be out-of-order on any given day.

About the *Resampling Stats* Software

Thanks to the personal computer and the program language RESAMPLING STATS, we now have a much faster way of solving problems with resampling. One may also use standard computer languages like BASIC or PASCAL to write programs that duplicate the simulation steps described above. Such programs are quite cumbersome, however, and sometimes result in reliance on pre-written canned routines which are as mysterious as formulae. RESAMPLING STATS is a small set of simple, intuitive commands that get the job done quickly and efficiently, and with total understanding on the part of the user.

The core of the program to solve the above problem begins with this command to the computer:

GENERATE 20 1,10 A

This command orders the computer to randomly GENERATE twenty numbers between "1" and "10." Inasmuch as each truck has a 1 in 10 chance of being defective, we decide arbitrarily that a "1" stands for a defective truck, and the other nine numbers (from "2" to "10") stand for a non-defective truck. The command orders the computer to store the results of the random drawing in the location in the computer's memory that we give a name such as "A" or "ZILCH".

The next key element in the core of the program is

COUNT A =1 B

This command orders the computer to COUNT the number of "1's" among the twenty numbers that are in location A following the random drawing carried out by the GENERATE operation. The result of the COUNT will be somewhere between 0 and 20, the number of trucks that might be out-of-order on a given day. The result is then placed in another location labeled B.

Now let us place the GENERATE and COUNT commands within the entire program that we use to solve this problem, which is:

25

Program "TRUCKS"

REPEAT 400	Repeat the simulation 400 times
GENERATE 20 1,10 A	Generate 20 numbers, each between 1 and 10, and put them in vector A. Each number will represent a truck, and we let 1 represent a defective truck.
COUNT A =1 B	Count the number of defective trucks, put the result in B.
SCORE B Z	Keep track of each trial's results in Z.
END	End this trial, then go back and repeat the process until all 400 trials are complete, then proceed.
COUNT Z > 3 K	Determine how many trials resulted in more than 3 trucks out of order.
DIVIDE K 400 L	Convert to a proportion.
PRINT L	Print the result.

The SCORE statement that follows the COUNT operation simply keeps track of the results of each trial, placing the number of defective trucks that occur in each trial in a location that we usually call "Z." This is done in each of the 400 trials that we make, and the result eventually is a "vector" with a 400 numbers in it.

In order to make 400 repetitions of our experiment -- we could have decided to make a thousand or some other number of repetitions -- we put REPEAT 400 before the GENERATE, COUNT, and SCORE statements that constitute a single trial. Then we complete each repetition "loop" with END.

26

Since our aim is to count the number of days in which more than 3 defective trucks occur, we use the COUNT command to count how many times in the 400 days recorded in our SCORE vector at the end of the 400 trials more than 3 defects occurred, and we place the result in still another location "K." This gives us the total number of days where 4 or more defective trucks are seen to occur. Then we DIVIDE the number in "K" by 400, the number of trials. Thus we obtain an estimate of the chance, expressed as a probability between 0 and 1, that 4 or more trucks will be defective on a given day. And we store that result in a location that we decide to call "L," so that it will be there when the computer receives the next command to PRINT that result.

Can you see how each of the operations that the computer carries out are analogous to the operations that you yourself executed when you solved this problem using a ten-sided spinner or a random number table? This is exactly the procedure that we will use to solve every problem in probability and statistics that we must deal with. Either we will use a device such as coins or a random number table as an analogy for the physical process we are interested in (trucks becoming defective, in this case), or we will simulate the analogy on the computer using the RESAMPLING STATS program.

Simple as it is, the RESAMPLING STATS program called "TRUCKS" may seem not so simple to you. But it is infinitely simpler than the older conventional approach to such problems that has routinely been taught to students for decades.

In the standard approach the student learns to choose and solve a formula. Doing the algebra and arithmetic is quick and easy. The difficulty is in choosing the correct formula. Unless you are a professional mathematician, it may take you quite a while to arrive at the correct formula -- considerable hard thinking, and perhaps some digging in textbooks. More important than the labor, however, is that you may come up with the wrong formula, and hence obtain the wrong answer. Most students who have had a standard course in probability and statistics are quick to tell you that it is not easy to find the correct formula, even immediately after finishing a course on the subject. And after leaving school later on it is even harder to choose the right formula. Even many people who have taught statistics at the university level (including this writer) must look at a book to get the correct formula for a problem as simple as the trucks, and even then we are not always sure of the right answer. This is the grave disadvantage of the standard approach.

In the past few decades, the resampling method has come to be used extensively in scientific research. But in contrast to the material in this book, the method has mostly been used in situations so complex that mathematical methods have not yet been developed to handle them. Here are examples of such situations:

1. For a rocket aimed at the moon, calculating the correct flight route involves a great many variables, too many to solve with formulae. Hence, the resampling method is used.

2. The Navy might want to know how long the average ship will have to wait for dock facilities. The time of completion varies from ship to ship, and the number of ships waiting in line for dockwork varies over time. This problem can be handled quite easily with the experimental resampling method, but formal mathematical analysis would be difficult or impossible.

3. What are the best tactics in baseball? Should one bunt? Should one put the best hitter up first, or later? By trying out various tactics with dice or random numbers, Earnshaw Cook, (in his book Percentage Baseball), found that it is best never to bunt, and the highest-average hitter should be put up first, in contrast to usual practice. Finding this answer would not be possible with the analytic method.

4. What search pattern will best help a ship searching for a school of fish? Trying out "models" of various search patterns with the resampling method can provide a fast answer.

5. What strategy in the game of Monopoly will be most likely to win? The resampling method systematically plays many games (with a computer) testing various strategies to find the best one.

But those five examples are all complex problems. Resampling breaks new ground by using this method for simple rather than complex problems, and in teaching beginning rather than advanced students to solve problems this way. (Here it is necessary to emphasize that the resampling method is used to solve the problems themselves rather than as a demonstration device to teach the notions found in the standard conventional approach. Resampling simulation has been used in elementary courses in the past, but only to demonstrate the operation of the analytical mathematical ideas. That is very different than using the resampling approach to solve problems themselves, as is done here.)

Like all new methods, resampling has both advantages and disadvantages. The main disadvantage is that while you are learning the resampling method you are not learning the older standard method. If you intend to go on to advanced statistical work, your introduction to the older standard conventional approach may therefore be slowed somewhat. However, the older standard method can be learned alongside resampling methods, and your introduction to the conventional method may thereby be made much more meaningful.

A longer discussion of the advantages and disadvantages of the resampling method for beginning students is given below in "A Note to the Teacher."

A NOTE TO THE TEACHER

Usually the textbook writer addresses the teacher in a preface or introduction. I have instead put this note after Chapter 2 for two reasons: First, its content depends upon Chapter 2, and second, some students might find it interesting or useful at this point.

Evidence that the Resampling Approach Works Well

These four criteria can help judge whether a new approach to solving statistics problems is sound: 1) Does the method produce correct answers? 2) Can beginning students produce the correct answers? 3)

Can the method be <u>learned rapidly</u>? 4) Is learning the method an <u>enjoyable experience</u>? This section offers evidence that the resampling method of solving statistics problems passes all these tests with flying colors.

1. <u>Correct answers</u>. It can be proven mathematically that the resampling method yields "unbiased" estimates of the true answers. The underlying reason is that the resampling method itself takes an unbiased sample of all the possible outcomes of the process that one is interested in. To illustrate this rather abstruse formal statement, let's say that we want to know the probability that a person will get five or more spades in a bridge hand of thirteen cards. One way to solve this problem would be to laboriously produce every single possible different arrangement of the fifty-two cards divided into four hands. Then among all these possible arrangements one would count how many hands have five or more spades; the ratio of the number of hands with five or more spades divided by the total number of hands with all possible arrangements would be an estimate of the probability that in any given single hand one would get five or more spades.

The traditional analytical approach to the problem, instead of laboriously producing each arrangement, is to calculate <u>analytically</u> how many possible arrangements of 52 cards there are among the four hands, then calculate analytically the number of possible hands that have five or more spades. The ratio is then the answer sought. The conventional approach is perfect, of course, except for the enormous difficulty of learning how to obtain the right formula.

In the resampling method we <u>experimentally</u> produce a fairly large number of the possible outcomes, though nowhere near all of the outcomes that are possible. Furthermore, we do not need to have any rules that teach us how to produce all the possible arrangements; that is automatically taken care of when we simply deal out the four hands in a random fashion. When we deal out hands and count the proportion with five or more spades, we are taking an unbiased sample of all the possible arrangements. Of course we may get some arrangements more than once, but that is quite all right. Hence the answer that we get with the resampling method is, on the average, a perfectly sound answer to the question we seek to answer.

If we do not make enough experimental trials with the resampling method, of course, the answer that we arrive at may be inexact. For example, if we produce only ten bridge hands experimentally we could by chance be somewhat too high or too low in our estimate of the probability of five or more spades. But with a reasonably large number of experimental bridge hands we can arrive at an answer that is close enough for any purpose. A few years ago, there were some problems for which one could not easily do enough experimental trials by hand to reach a satisfactory answer. But now if the problem demands a great many experimental trials, we turn to a computer to do the dirty work for us -- dealing out the bridge hands, in this case. With a computer we can always do enough trials to get an answer close enough to the true answer to be satisfactory. Therefore we can assert that the resampling method passes the test of getting sound answers to questions about probability and statistics.

2. <u>Do students learn to reach sound answers</u>? Actual classroom experiments show that students successfully produce correct answers to problems in probability and statistics with this method. For example, I taught a class of second-year and third-year university students from a great many social-science disciplines with <u>both</u> the older standard method and the resampling method. All problems that were treated by the resampling method in class were also demonstrated by analytic methods, whereas many problems were solved by analytic methods that were <u>not</u> treated in class by the resampling method. Therefore, analytic methods had a very large advantage over the resampling method in student time and attention, both in reading and in class.

On the final exam, there were four questions that the student could <u>choose</u> whether to answer by analytic methods or by resampling. The choices of methods by the students gives an indication of the usefulness of the resampling method. These were the results: a) Almost every student used the resampling method for at least one question. In total, almost half of the answers given were done by the resampling method (41 of 84). b) There was a slightly greater propensity for the students who did better on the examination as a whole to do a larger proportion of problems by the resampling method. c) Analytic and resampling methods were both used on each question by some students. d) The grades that the students received were somewhat higher on the questions answered with the resampling method than on those questions answered with analytic methods.

In a Ph.D. thesis studying junior college students who had little aptitude for mathematics, Shevokas (1974) taught the resampling approach to two groups of students (one with and one without computer), and the conventional approach to a "control" group. [1] She then tested the groups on problems that could be done either analytically or by resampling. Students taught with the resampling method were able to solve more than twice as many problems correctly as students who were taught the conventional approach (Shevokas, 1974, pp. 118-119).

Atkinson twice taught the resampling approach and the conventional approach to matched classes in general mathematics at a small college. The students who learned the resampling method did better on the final exam with questions about general statistical understanding. They also did much better solving actual problems, producing 73 percent more correct answers than the conventionally-taught control group (Atkinson, 1975, pp. 60-79, 81, 82).

These experiments are strong evidence that students who learn the resampling method are able to solve problems better than conventionally taught students.

3. How fast do students learn to solve problems with the resampling method? In my university class, only a small fraction of total class time -- perhaps an eighth - was devoted to the resampling method as compared to seven-eighths spent on the conventional method. Yet, the tested students learned to solve problems more correctly, and solved more problems, with the resampling method than with the conventional method. This suggests that resampling is learned much faster than the conventional method.

In the Shevokas and Atkinson experiments the same amount of time was devoted to both methods but the resampling method achieved better results. So, in those experiments the resampling method is at least as fast as the conventional method, and probably considerably faster.

32

4. Is the resampling method interesting and enjoyable?
Shevokas asked her groups of students for their opinions and attitudes
about the section of the course devoted to statistics and probability.
The attitudes of the students who learned the resampling method were
far more positive -- they found the work much more interesting and
enjoyable -- than the attitudes of the students taught with the standard
method (Shevokas, 1974, pp. 135 and 145). And the attitudes of the
resampling students toward mathematics in general improved during the
weeks of instruction while the attitudes of the students taught
conventionally changed for the worse (ibid., p. 146) Shevokas summed
up the students' reactions as follows:

> "Students in the experimental (resampling) classes were
> much more enthusiastic during class hours than those in
> the control group, they responded more, made more
> suggestions, and seemed to be much more involved"
> (ibid., p. 163)."

Another example: Gideon Keren taught the resampling
approach for just six hours to 14- and 15-year old high school students
in Jerusalem. The students knew that they would not be tested on the
materials in any way. Yet, Keren reported that the students were very
much interested. And as the instructor he enjoyed teaching this material
because the students were enjoying themselves. Proof that the material
interested them: between the second and third class, two students asked
to join the class though it was their free period.

Atkinson's resampling students had "more favorable opinions,
and more favorable changes in opinions" about mathematics generally
than the conventionally taught students (Atkinson, 1975, first draft, pp.
62-63) according to an attitude questionnaire. And with respect to the
study of statistics in particular, the resampling students had much more
favorable attitudes (ibid., pp. 98-99) and seemed to be having a very
good time.

This evidence that the resampling approach is sound is intended
to give you confidence. But for you the ultimate test of this method is
whether your students prefer it to the conventional method (or to no
method at all) for problems on examinations and in their lives.

For Whom and When Is the Resampling Approach Good?

There are several groups of people for whom learning resampling statistics makes sense:

1.   <u>People who may use statistics sometime in their career but who will not be professional statisticians</u>. This includes people who work in or around the social sciences such as social workers, scientists at the master's or BA level who may work on social-science (or biological-science) projects, as well as market researchers and engineers.

2.   <u>People who will be "consumers" of statistics rather than "producers" of statistics</u>. This includes executives and other administrators who read research reports. People who will be consumers of statistics ought also to learn the terms used in the standard approach as, for example "the level of significance." These terms are explained in this book.

3.   <u>Students who intend to continue in statistics and mathematics</u>. Such students benefit from a study of the resampling approach because it gives them an excellent intuitive feel for many concepts that they will use later. When doing problems with the resampling method, one gets an excellent feeling for the nature of probability and statistics.

Should the Resampling Approach Be Taught by Itself, or Along with the Conventional Method?

The approach as described in this text is complete in itself for the study of probability and statistics at the elementary level. But it also may be used along with a traditional text that teaches the standard conventional method. For those readers who will use the resampling approach together with the standard conventional method, some guideposts for coordination of the two methods are given throughout the book.

About Teaching Resampling

The skilled teacher of statistics may feel that conventional statistics can be taught with sufficient effectiveness so that there is no need to teach and use the resampling method. Putting aside for the moment the special advantages of the resampling method, let us meet this argument on its own ground.

It is an unfortunate fact that most conventional teaching of statistics is a miserable failure. And that is why I originally came to teach the resampling method. I was then teaching a course in research methods at the University of Illinois to graduate students from a variety of social-science disciplines. All the students had studied statistics at the University of Illinois or elsewhere. But when the time came to apply even the simplest statistical ideas and tests in their research projects, almost all the students were sadly lost. Their statistics courses had plainly failed to equip them with the simplest usable statistical tools. It was to remedy their inability to do statistics that I turned to teaching the resampling method.

To repeat, perhaps conventional statistics can be taught successfully. But in practice it usually is not taught successfully. That is reason enough to turn to a method that does produce good results.

The resampling method is not offered as a successor to analytic methods. Rather, it can be underpinning for analytic teaching to help students understand analytic methods better. And it is also a workable and easily taught alternative for students who will never study analytic methods to the point of practical mastery -- and this includes most students at all levels. It may be especially useful for the introduction to statistics of mathematically disadvantaged students. (But please do not infer from this that the method is intellectually inferior; the method is logically quite acceptable and intuitively instructive for all students).

Please understand that the resampling methods used here really are intended as alternatives to conventional analytic methods in actual problem-solving practice. It must be emphasized that these methods are not pedagogical devices for improving the teaching of conventional methods. This is completely different than the past use of the resampling methods to help teach sampling theory, the binomial theorem and the central limit theorem. The point that is usually hardest to convey to teachers of statistics is that the method suggested here really is a complete break in conventional thinking, rather than a supplement to it or an aid in teaching it. The simple resampling methods described here are complete in themselves for handling those many problems in probability and statistics which they can handle.

That the resampling method <u>can</u> be complete unto itself-- though it does not <u>need</u> to be -- is harder to grasp because it <u>seems</u> to call into question the worth of one's stock of professional knowledge. But use of the resampling method does not, in fact, make obsolete one's present knowledge of statistics. Rather it complements the analytic approach, and the two can dovetail nicely in an elementary course. Or, learning the resampling method lays a useful base for the learning of analytic methods for those students who will press on later with analytic methods.

Lest this be unclear or seem to equivocate: where there is limited time, or where students will not be able to grasp conventional methods firmly, I advocate teaching the resampling approach, and perhaps that only. Where there is more time, and where students will be able to learn conventional methods, I advocate teaching resampling a) at the very beginning as an introduction to statistical thinking and practice, and b) afterwards teaching it together with conventional methods as alternatives to the same problem, to help students learn analytic methods and to give them an alternative tool for their use.

The method is not really <u>taught</u> by an instructor. Rather it is <u>learned</u> by the students. With a bit of guidance from the instructor, the students invent, from scratch, resampling methods of doing statistics problems. For example, at the beginning of an illustrative first class, the instructor asks, "What are the chances that if you have four children three of them will be girls?" A few students do some calculations without success (in a naive class). The students then say they don't know how to get the answer. The instructor then presses the class to think of <u>some</u> way to find the answer. Someone suggests in jest that everyone in the class should go out and have four children. The instructor chooses to take this seriously. He says that this is a very good suggestion, though it has some obvious drawbacks. Someone suggests substituting a coin for a birth. This raises the issue of whether it is reasonable to approximate a 106:100 event with a 50-50 coin, and what is reasonable under various conditions. The instructor points out that the class still has no answer. Someone suggests that each student throw four coins. Someone else amends this by saying four flips of one coin is just as good. The instructor questions whether the two methods are equivalent, and the class eventually agrees that they are. Finally, each student runs a trial, the data are collected, and an estimate is made. Someone considers how good the estimate is. Someone else suggests that the experiment be conducted several more times to see how much variation there is.

The meaning of the concept "chances" comes up in the discussion, and "probability" is defined pragmatically. By this process of self-discovery, students develop useful operating definitions of other necessary concepts such as "universe," "trial," "estimate," and so on. And together they invent -- after false starts and class corrections -- sound approaches to easy and not-so-easy problems in probability and statistics. For example, with a bit of guidance an average university class can be brought to reinvent such devices as a resampling version of Fisher's randomization test. (The flexibility and range of such resampling methods was shown in an early report [Simon, 1969] in illustrative solutions to problems ranging from permutations to correlation to randomization tests.)

In this manner the students learn more than how to do problems. They gain the excitement of true intellectual discovery. And they come to understand something of the nature of mathematics and its creation.

An excerpted example of the actual discussion of a class learning with resampling is reproduced in Appendix 1 at the end of the book.

Of course, this "discovery" method of teaching can cause problems for some teachers. It requires that you react spontaneously and let the discussion find its own path, rather than having everything prepared in advance. For some teachers it may take some practice.

Others may never find it congenial. But for the teacher who is open and responsive and a bit inventive, teaching the resampling method in this fashion is wonderfully exciting. Perhaps most exciting is to see ordinary students inventing solutions to problems that conventional probability theory did not discover for many centuries.

The openness of resampling learning also bothers some students, especially at first. They miss the confidence they get from a notebook full of well-organized cut-and-dried formulae, and the lack of structure worries some students. But after a few weeks, the average student comes to like the resampling approach better, as the controlled experiments of Shevokas (1974) and Atkinson (1975) show.

Advantages and Disadvantages of the Resampling Method

With card and dice experiments one can make statistical tests without the mathematical theory of probability. But figuring the answer analytically is often quicker, especially for problems with many observations. For example, imagine that you want to know how often you will get two aces if you deal a hand of only two cards. A random experiment would take a while, but one can figure the answer in a hurry by multiplying 4/52 x 3/51 which tells us that, on the average, we shall get two aces in a hand of two cards once in 220 hands.

Though analytical methods may produce an answer quicker than the resampling method, a person who does not expect to use probability statistics very often might find that, in the long run, it is more efficient to spend a bit of extra time on doing resampling trials rather than a lot of time in studying the mathematical methods. On the other hand, anyone who plans to work scientific research should eventually study analytic statistics, especially because that study deepens one's intuition about scientific and mathematical relationships.

An important advantage of the resampling method is that everything that you do is very explicit, and you must think through each step. Such discipline reduces the probability of erroneous calculations from blindly plugging in the wrong method and formula. Moreover, the learning and practicing of this approach aids problem solving in general. Formerly, it was a disadvantage of the resampling method executed by hand that large sample sizes were clumsy to work with, especially when the simplest probabilities are small; for example, formerly it was difficult to do a resampling experiment with data on the viewership of educational television stations because the potential audience is many thousands while the probability of a given person watching may be only 1 in 1,000. But the need to test usually arises only when the samples are small; with large masses of data the conclusions are obvious without probability statistics. Furthermore, RESAMPLING STATS and the computer easily handle large masses of data.

Another advantage of the resampling method with the computer program RESAMPLING STATS is that it serves as a painless introduction to the use of computers and computer programming. Such basic concepts as IF and looping are learned without special instruction because they are seen to be necessary for repeated resampling trials. And general notions such as booting up, menus, and the operating system also are learned without fuss, as natural parts of the process, simply because this is what the students find themselves doing. Fear of computers also is rapidly dispelled in this environment.

Let us consider some criticisms of the use of resampling methods to solve simple problems. The first objection is the easiest to meet -- that the estimates are inaccurate. Notably resampling sample sizes must be large enough for any desired level of accuracy. In most situations, an adequate sample of random numbers can be drawn in a few minutes. If not, it is easy to program any of these procedures onto any computer using RESAMPLING STATS, and thereby obtain samples of huge sizes in seconds. With RESAMPLING STATS, even probabilities close to 0 or 1 can be estimated accurately in a short span of time. And students can do these problems with programming without difficulty.

Additionally, students who use this method quickly grasp the importance of inaccuracy due to sampling error as they observe the variation in their resampling samples. This causes them to worry about it -- which is the most important learning of all. Then the students increase their resampling samples in size until they reach acceptable levels of accuracy.

A more weighty objection is that this sort of teaching is obscurantist, anti-intellectual, and likely to limit the student's advance into formal mathematical analysis. There are several responses to this objection:

1. There are many students who will never go forward with the study of statistics and mathematics, even if they are never exposed to this instruction. For these students this powerful engine of problem-solving is an important educational bonus.

2. This instruction interests many students. I will wager that it pushes more students forward into further study than it stops.

3. Perhaps most important, this instruction is of great value to those who <u>will</u> study statistics and probability. The procedure by which the student must explicitly structure problems in this method is <u>also</u> necessary when problems are solved analytically -- but the structuring process is too often done implicitly or without awareness in analytic work, which often leads to the wrong model or unsound choice of a cookbook formula. This instruction is therefore of great value in teaching students what analytic methods are good for, and how to use them correctly.

NOTES:

[1]   Professor Kenneth Travers has been responsible for the study by Shevokas and that by Atkinson described below, as well as for other research on this subject at the University of Illinois College of Education.

CHAPTER 3

BASIC CONCEPTS IN PROBABILITY AND STATISTICS

INTRODUCTION

THE NATURE AND MEANING OF PROBABILITY

CONDITIONAL AND UNCONDITIONAL PROBABILITIES

THE CONCEPT OF INDEPENDENT EVENTS

SAMPLES AND UNIVERSES

THE DISTINCTION BETWEEN "PROBABILITY THEORY"
AND "INFERENTIAL STATISTICS"

INTRODUCTION

This chapter discusses what is meant by some key terms such as "probability", "conditional" and "unconditional" probability, "independence", "sample", and "universe". It discusses the nature and the usefulness of the concept of probability as used here, and touches on the source of basic estimates of probability that are the raw material of analyses. And it distinguishes between probability theory and inferential statistics. (Descriptive statistics, the other main branch of statistics, was discussed in the previous chapter).

THE NATURE AND MEANING OF PROBABILITY

What does the term "probability" mean? To say that an event has a high or low probability is simply to make a statement that forecasts the future. In practice, probability is stated as a decimal number between "0" and "1," such that "0" means you estimate that there is no chance of the event happening, and "1" means you are certain the event will happen. A probability estimate of .2 indicates that you think there is twice as great a chance of the events happening as if you had estimated a probability of .1. The idea of probability arises when you are not sure about what will happen about a future event -- that is, when you do not have enough information and therefore can only estimate. For example, if someone asks you what your name is, you do not use the concept of probability to answer; you know the answer. To be sure, there is some chance that you do not know your own name, but for all practical purposes you can be quite sure of the answer. If someone asks you who will win tomorrow's ball game, however, there is a chance that you will be wrong, no matter what you say. Whenever the situation is such that there is a chance that you could be wrong, the concept of probability can help you.

A probability statement is always about the future. But often one does not know what the likelihoods really are for future events, except in the case of a gambler playing black on an honest roulette wheel, or an insurance company issuing a policy on an event with which it has had a lot of experience, such as a life insurance policy. Therefore, we must make guesses about the likelihoods, using various common-sense devices. All these techniques should be thought of as proxies for the actual probability. For example, if NASA Mission Control simulates what will probably happen if a valve is turned aboard an Apollo space craft, the result on the ground is not the real probability that it will happen in space, but rather a proxy for the real probability. If a manager looks at the sales of radios in the last two Decembers, and on that basis guesses the likelihood that he will run out of stock if he orders 200 radios, then the last two years' experience is serving as a proxy for future experience. If a sales manager just "intuits" that the odds are 3 to 1 (a probability of .75) that the main competitor will not meet a price cut, then all his past experience summed into his intuition is a proxy for the probability that it will really happen. Whether any proxy is a good or bad one depends on the wisdom of the person choosing the proxy and making the probability estimates.

The concept of probability helps you to answer the question, "What are the chances that ...?"[2] The purpose of this discussion of probability statistics is to help you become a good bettor, to help you make sound appraisals of true and untrue conclusions (or, in terms of decision theory, to help you decide which alternative you should bet on). The concept of probability is especially useful when one has a "sample" from a "universe" and wants to know the probability of various degrees of likeness between the sample and the universe. (The "universe" is the "population" of events you are "sampling" from, as discussed below.) Perhaps the universe of your study is all high school seniors in 1988. You might then want to know the probability that the universe's average SAT score, for example, will not differ from your sample's average SAT by more than some arbitrary number of SAT points, say, ten points.

It is confusing and unnecessary to inquire what probability "really is." Various definitions of the term are useful in particular contexts (see Ayer, 1965; Schlaifer, 1961, Chapter 1). This book contains many examples of the use of probability, and, as you work with them, you will develop a sound feeling for the concept. The following two definitions (which are not always compatible) may be helpful to start you off:

1. The probability that an event will take place or that a statement is true can be said to correspond to the odds at which you would bet that the event will take place. (Notice a shortcoming of this definition: You might be willing to accept a five-dollar bet at 2-1 odds that your team will win the game, but you might be unwilling to bet a hundred dollars at the same odds.)

2. The probability of an event can be said to be the proportion of times that the event has taken place in the past, usually based on a long series of trials. Insurance companies use this type of definition when they estimate the probability that a thirty-five-year-old postman will die during a period for which he wants to buy an insurance policy. (Notice this shortcoming: Sometimes you must bet upon events that have never or only infrequently taken place before, and so you cannot reasonably reckon the proportion of times they occurred one way or the other in the past.)

You have been using the concept of probability all your life, in practically every decision you have ever made and in every conclusion you have ever drawn. You place your blanket on the beach where there is a low probability of someone's kicking sand on you; you bet heavily on a poker hand when there is a high probability that you have the best hand; a hospital decides not to buy another ambulance when the administrator figures that there is a low probability that all the other ambulances will ever be in use at once.

How does one estimate a probability? First, let us consider how one can estimate an ordinary garden variety of probability, which is called an "unconditional" probability. Several ways to estimate an unconditional probability can be illustrated with an example from poker. [3] What is the probability of drawing an even-numbered spade from a deck of poker cards?

1.   Experience: The first possible source for an estimate of the probability of drawing an even-numbered spade is <u>experience</u>. If you have watched card games casually from time to time, you might guess at the proportion of times you have seen even-numbered spades appear, and you might guess "about 1 in 15" or "about 1 in 6" (which is correct) or something like that. (The actual probability is 6 to 52, of course.) You might make an estimate based on your experience if someone asked you the probability that two cards of the same denomination will turn up in the same hand of five cards dealt from a poker deck. General information and experience are also the source for estimating the probability that your team will win tomorrow, that war will break out next year, or that a United States astronaut will reach Mars before a Soviet astronaut. You simply put together all your relevant prior experience and knowledge and make a guess.

2.   Experiment: The second possible source of probability estimates is empirical scientific investigation with repeated trials of the phenomenon -- called a "frequency series". In the case of the even-numbered spade, the empirical scientific procedure is to shuffle the cards, deal one, record whether or not the card is an even-number spade, replace the card, and repeat the steps a good many times. The proportions of times you observe an even-numbered spade come up is a probability estimate based on a frequency series. You might reasonably ask why we do not just <u>count</u> the number of even-numbered spades in the deck of fifty two cards. No reason at all. But that procedure would not work if you wanted to estimate the probability of a batter getting a hit or a cigarette lighter lighting.

Observation of frequency series might help you to estimate the probability that a machine will turn out a defective part or that a child can memorize four nonsense syllables correctly in one attempt. You watch and record the results of repeated trials of exactly the same event.

There is no logical difference between the sort of probability that the life insurance company estimates on the basis of its "frequency series" of past death rates, and the salesman's seat-of-the-pants estimate of what the competition will do. [4] No frequency series can speak for itself in a perfectly objective manner. Many judgments go into compiling every frequency series, in deciding which frequency series to use for an estimate, and in choosing which part of the frequency series to use. For example, should the insurance company use only its records from last year, which will be too few to give as many data as would be liked, or should it also use death records from years further back, when conditions were slightly different together with data from other sources? In view of the necessarily subjective nature of probability estimates, the reader may prefer to talk about "degrees of belief" instead of probabilities. That's fine, just a long as it is understood that we operate with degrees of belief in exactly the same way as we operate with probabilities; the two terms are working synonyms. (Of course, no two events are exactly the same. But under many circumstances they are practically the same, and science is only interested in such "practical" considerations.)

3. **Counting the possibilities:** A third source of probability estimates is counting the possibilities. For example, by examination of an ordinary die one can determine that there are six different possible numbers that can come up. One can then determine that the probability of getting a "1" or a "2," say, is 2/6 = 1/3, because two of six possibilities are "1" or "2." One can similarly determine that there are two possibilities of getting a "1" plus a "6" out of thirty-six possibilities when rolling two dice, a probability of 2/36 = 1/18.

Determining probabilities by counting has two requirements: that the possibilities all be known (and therefore limited), and few enough to be studied easily; and that the probability of each particular possibility be known, for example, that the probabilities of all sides of the dice coming up are equal, that is, equal to 1/6.

4.   Mathematical shortcuts: A fourth source of probability estimates is mathematical calculations. If one knows by other means that the probability of a spade is 1/4 and the probability of an even-numbered card is 6/13, one can then calculate that the probability of turning up an even-numbered spade is 6/52 (that is, 1/4 x 6/13). If one knows that the probability of a spade is 1/4 and the probability of a heart is 1/4, then one can calculate that the probability of getting a heart or a spade is 1/2 (that is 1/4 + 1/4). The point here is not the particular calculation procedures, but rather that one can often calculate the desired probability on the basis of already-known probabilities.

It is possible to estimate probabilities with mathematical calculation only if one knows by other means the probabilities of some related events. For example, there is no possible way of mathematically calculating that a child will memorize four nonsense syllables correctly in one attempt; empirical knowledge is necessary.

CONDITIONAL AND UNCONDITIONAL PROBABILITIES

Two kinds of probability statements must be distinguished, conditional and unconditional.

Let's use a football example to explain conditional and unconditional probabilities. In the year this is being written, the University of Maryland has an unpromising football team. Someone may nevertheless ask what chance the team has of winning the post season game at the bowl to which only the best team in the University of Maryland's league is sent. One may say that if by some miracle the University of Maryland does get to the bowl, its chance would be a bit less than 50-50 -- say, .40. That is, the probability of its winning, conditional on getting to the bowl is .40. But the chance of its getting to the bowl at all is very low, perhaps .01. If so, the unconditional probability of winning at the bowl is the probability of its getting there multiplied by the probability of winning if it gets there; that is, .01 x .40 = .004. (It would be even better to say that .004 is the probability of winning conditional only on having a team, there being a league, and so on, all of which seem almost sure things.) Every probability is conditional on many things -- that war does not break out, that the sun continues to rise, and so on. But if all those unspecified conditions are very sure, and can be taken for granted, we talk of the probability as unconditional.

A conditional probability is a statement that the probability of an event is such-and-such _if_ something else is so-and-so; it is the "if" that makes a probability statement conditional. True, in _some_ sense all probability statements are conditional; for example, the probability of an even-numbered spade is 6/52 _if_ the deck is a poker deck and not necessarily if it is a pinochle deck or Tarot deck. But we ignore such conditions for most purposes.

Most of the use of probability in the social sciences is _conditional_ probability. All hypothesis-testing statistics are conditional probabilities.

This is the typical conditional-probability question used in social-science statistics: What is the probability of obtaining this sample S (by chance) _if_ the sample were taken from universe A? For example, what is the probability of getting a sample of five children with I.Q.s over 100 _by chance_ in a sample randomly chosen from the universe of children whose average I.Q. is 100?

The first source of such conditional-probability statements is examination of the frequency series generated by universes like the conditional universe. For example, assume that we are considering a universe of children that average an I.Q. of 100. Write down "over 100" and "under 100" respectively on a big bunch of slips of paper, put them into a hat, draw five slips several times, and see how often the first five slips drawn are all over 100. This is the resampling method of estimating probabilities.

The second source of such conditional-probability statements is mathematical calculation. For example, if half the slips in the hat have numbers under 100 and half over 100, the probability of getting five in a row above 100 is $.5^5$, that is $.5 \times .5 \times .5 \times .5 \times .5$. But if you do not know the proper mathematical formula, you can come very close with the resampling method as close as you like.

How may one estimate probabilities wisely? Sound estimation depends largely upon gathering evidence well. It may also depend on some skill in adjusting one's probability estimates to make them internally consistent.

THE CONCEPT OF INDEPENDENT EVENTS

A key concept in the use of probability and statistics is that of independence of two events. Two events are said to be "independent" when one of them does not seem to have any relation to the other. If I flip a coin that I know from other evidence is a fair coin, and I get a head, the chance of then getting another head is still 50-50 (one in two, or one to one.) And, if I flip a coin ten times and get heads the first nine times, the probability of getting a head on the tenth flip is still 50-50. This is why the concept of independence is characterized by the phrase "The coin has no memory." (Actually the matter is a bit more complicated. If you had previously flipped the coin many times and knew it to be a fair coin, then the odds would still be 50-50, even after nine heads. But, if you had never seen the coin before, the run of nine heads might reasonably make you doubt that the coin was a fair one.)

Nevertheless, people commonly make the mistake of treating independent events as non-independent, perhaps from superstitious belief. Roulette gamblers say that the wheel is "due" to come up red. And sportswriters make a living out of interpreting various sequences of athletic events that occur by chance, and talk of teams that are "due" to win because of the "Law of Averages." For example, if Don Mattingly goes to bat four times without a hit, all of us (including trained statisticians who really know better) feel that he is "due" to get a hit and that the probability of his doing so is very high -- higher that is, than his season's average. The so-called "Law of Averages" implies no such thing, of course.

Events are often independent in subtle ways. A boy may telephone one of several girls chosen at random. But, if he calls the same girl again (or if he does not call her again), the second event is

48

not likely to be independent of the first, and the probability of his calling her is <u>different</u> after he has gone out with her once than before he went out with her.

This observation suggests a more careful definition of independence: If the occurrence of the first event does not change this probability that the second event will occur, then the events are independent.

SAMPLES AND UNIVERSES

The terms "sample" and "universe" (or "population") [5] were used above without definition. But now these terms must be defined.

For our purposes, a "sample" is a collection of observations for which you have data with which you are going to work. Almost any set of observations for which you have data constitutes a sample. (You might or might not call a complete census a sample.)

For every sample there must also be a universe "behind" it. But "universe" is harder to define, partly because it is often an <u>imaginary</u> concept. A universe is the collection of things or people <u>that you want to say that your sample was taken from</u>. A universe can be finite and well defined -- "all live holders of the Congressional Medal of Honor", "all presidents of major universities", "all billion-dollar corporations in the United States". Of course, these finite universes may not be easy to pin down; for instance, what is a "major university"? And these universes may contain some elements that are difficult to find; for instance, some Congressional Medal winners may have left the country, and there may not be any public records on some billion-dollar corporations.

Infinite universes are harder to understand, and it is often difficult to decide which universe is appropriate for a given purpose. For example, if you are studying a sample of schizophrenics, what is the universe from which the sample comes? Depending on your purposes, the appropriate universe might be all schizophrenics now alive, or it might be all schizophrenics who might <u>ever</u> live. The latter concept of the universe of schizophrenics is <u>imaginary</u> because some of the universe does not exist. And it is _infinite_ because it goes on forever.

Not everyone likes this definition of "universe". Others prefer to think of a universe, not as the collection of people or things that you _want_ to say your sample was taken from, but as the collection that the sample was _actually_ taken from. This latter view equates the universe to the "sampling frame" (the actual list or set of elements you sample from) which is always finite and existent. The definition of universe offered here is simply the most practical, in my opinion.

THE DISTINCTION BETWEEN "PROBABILITY THEORY" AND "INFERENTIAL STATISTICS"

The term "probability theory" refers to situations in which you know the nature of the system you are working with, and you wish to estimate the probability that the system will produce one or more _particular events_. For example, you can assume you know from the start the nature of a deck of bridge cards, and you want to estimate, say, the probability that such a deck with 13 spades among 52 cards will produce ten spades in the first thirteen cards dealt.

In contrast, the term "inferential statistics" refers to situations in which you do _not_ know the nature of the system you are dealing with, and you want to _infer_ the nature of the system from the evidence in hand. For example, someone may deal 10 spades to you in the first 13 cards, and you -- not knowing what kind of deck it is -- want to estimate how likely it is that the deck has only 13 spades among the 52 cards, or that it really has a larger proportion of spades.

To put it another way, in an inferential-statistics situation we want to _illuminate aspects of the system_; the mean and the median are examples of parameters that we wish to infer about an unknown system. In contrast, probability theory tells us about the _probability_ of particular occurrences within systems whose parameters we already know.

Clearly, probability theory is relevant to situations such as gambling with cards or dice where the physical nature of the system in known. It is also relevant to such business situations as life insurance, where the overall probabilities of dying at each age are well known from a great deal of prior experience. (Business situations in which one does not know the structure of the situation but is prepared to assume what it is can similarly be dealt with using probability theory.)

Inferential statistical thinking is particularly relevant for scientific investigations. In much of science the researcher tries to determine the nature of an unknown system from the evidence that he collects about it.

NOTES:

[1]   The material in this chapter is largely drawn from Simon (1969; 3rd edition with Paul Burstein, 1985).

[2]   A given probability may be expressed in terms of probability, odds, or chances, and I shall use all three terms to help familiarize you with them. If the chances are 1 in 10, the odds are 9 to 1, and the probability is .1. If the odds are 2 to 5, the chances are 5 in 7, and the probability is 5/7. If the odds are 99 to 1, the chances are 1 in 100, and the probability is .01. If the odds are 100 to 1, the chances are 1 in 101, and the probability is 1/101. "Likelihood" is a synonym for "probability".

[3]   I hope you are not offended by the references to gambling games in the discussion of statistics in this and other chapters. Not only was the theory of probability invented to answer questions about gambling games, but gambling games still provide useful examples.

[4]   At one time, some writers believed there was a difference between "objectively sharply defined" and "objectively vague" probabilities. Raiffa gives a clear example of why this is not so:

Suppose you are confronted with two options. In option 1, you must toss coin 1 (which is fair and true), guess heads or tails, and win $1.00 if you match and lose $1.00 if you fail to match. In option 2, you have a 50-50 chance of getting coin 2, which has two heads, or of getting coin 3, which has two tails. Not knowing whether you are tossing coin 2 or 3, you must call, toss, and get the payoffs as in option 1. With option 1, the probability of the toss coming out heads is .5; with option 2, the same probability is either 0 or 1, and since the chance of each in turn is .5, the probability of heads is ultimately .5 once again. Nothing is to be gained by saying that one .5 is sharply defined and that the other is fuzzy. Of course, if, and this is a big "if," you could experiment with the coin you will toss before you are obliged to declare, then the two options are manifestly asymmetrical. Barring this privilege, the two options are equivalent. (Raiffa, 1968, p. 108).

[5]   "Universe" and "population" are perfect synonyms in scientific research. I choose to use "universe" because it seems to have fewer confusing associations.

CHAPTER 4

ESTIMATING PROBABILITIES IN SYSTEMS WE UNDERSTAND

PROBABILITY THEORY, PART I

INTRODUCTION

AN INTRODUCTORY PROBLEM, Poker Hands

ANOTHER INTRODUCTORY POKER PROBLEM

SAMPLING FROM AN INFINITE UNIVERSE

EXAMPLE 4-1: Three Daughters Among Four Children (Two-Outcome Sampling with Equally Likely Outcomes; with Replacement)

A NOTE ON CLARIFYING AND LABELING PROBLEMS

EXAMPLE 4-2: Three or More Successful Basketball Shots in Five Attempts (Two-Outcome Sampling with Unequally Likely Outcomes, with Replacement -- A Binomial Experiment)

EXAMPLE 4-3: Four Successful Shots in a Row -- The Multiplication Rule

EXAMPLE 4-4: One in the Black, Two in the White, and No Misses in Three Archery Shots (Multiple-Outcome Sampling with Unequally Likely Outcomes, with Replacement)

THE ADDITION RULE

EXAMPLE 4-5: Eight or More Points in Seven Shots
EXAMPLE 4-6: The Birthday Problem
EXAMPLE 4-7: A Drunk's Random Walk

INTRODUCTION

This chapter deals with probability problems in which "the system is known." By "known" I mean that the probability of independent simple events is assumed to be known, and the problem is to determine the probability of various sequences or combinations of the simple events. The resampling method is then demonstrated with illustrative classic examples. In each problem, a single trial of the system is simulated with cards, dice, random numbers, or the computer, and then repeated to estimate the probability. We can obtain as accurate an estimate of the exact probability as we wish by increasing the number of trials. The key step in each problem is designing an experiment that accurately simulates the system in which we are interested.

This chapter begins the real resampling work. It deals with problems in probability theory, that is, situations where one wants to estimate the likelihood of one or more particular events when the basic structure and parameters of the system are known. In later chapters we move on to inferential statistics.

A few definitions:

Simple Event: An event such as a single flip of a coin, or the draw of a single card once. A simple event cannot be broken down into simpler events of a similar sort.

Composite Event: The combination of two or more simple events. Examples are three throws of a single coin; one throw of three coins at once; two spades being drawn in the first two cards dealt from the deck; the combination of exactly four heads occurring in the first four coin flips together with two spades occurring in the first two cards.

Experiment or Experimental Trial or Trial or Resampling Experiment: A randomly-generated composite event which has the same characteristics as the actual composite event in which we are interested (except that in inferential statistics the resampling experiment is generated with the "benchmark" or "null" universe rather than the "alternative" universe).

Parameter: A numerical property of a universe. For example, the "true" mean, and the range between largest and smallest members are two of its parameters.

Compound Probability: The probability that a composite event will occur.

Hypothesis: In inferential statistics, a statement or claim about a universe that can be tested and which you wish to investigate.

Testing: The process of investigating the validity of a hypothesis.

Benchmark (or null) hypothesis: A particular hypothesis chosen for convenience when testing hypotheses in inferential statistics. For example, we could test the hypothesis that there is no difference between a sample and a given universe, or between two samples, or that a parameter is less than or greater than a certain value.

AN INTRODUCTORY PROBLEM - Poker Hands

Let us now consider a pure problem in odds: What is the chance that the first five cards chosen from a deck of 52 (bridge/poker) cards will contain two (and only two) cards of the same denomination (two 3's for example)?

We shall estimate the odds the way that gamblers have estimated gambling odds for thousands of years. First, check that the deck is not a pinochle deck and is not missing any cards. (Overlooking such small but crucial matters often leads to errors in science.) Shuffle thoroughly until you are satisfied that the cards are randomly distributed. (It is surprisingly hard to shuffle well.) Then deal five cards, and mark down whether the hand does or does not contain a pair of the same denomination. At this point, we must decide whether three of a kind, four of a kind or two pairs meet our criterion for a pair. Since our criterion is "two and only two," we decide not to count them.

Then replace the five cards in the deck, shuffle, and deal again. Again mark down whether the hand contains one pair of the same denomination. Do this many times. Then count the number of hands with one pair, and figure the proportion (as a percentage) of all hands. In one series of 100 experiments, 44% of the hands contained one pair, and therefore .44 is our estimate of the probability that one pair will turn up in a poker hand.

Table 4-1												
Results of 100 Trials for the Problem "OnePair"												
Trial	1	2	3	4	5	6	7	8	9	10	11	12	13
Results	Y	Y	N	N	Y	Y	N	N	Y	N	N	Y	N
Trial	14	15	16	17	18	19	20	21	22	23	24	25	26
Results	N	Y	Y	Y	Y	Y	N	N	Y	N	Y	N	Y
Trial	27	28	29	30	31	32	33	34	35	36	37	38	39
Results	N	Y	N	Y	Y	N	Y	N	N	N	N	Y	N
Trial	40	41	42	43	44	45	46	47	48	49	50		
Results	N	N	N	N	Y	Y	Y	N	N	Y	N		
Subtotal: 23 Yes, 27 No = 46%													
Trial	51	52	53	54	55	56	57	58	59	60	61	62	63
Results	N	Y	N	N	Y	N	Y	Y	N	N	N	Y	Y
Trial	64	65	66	67	68	69	70	71	72	73	74	75	76
Results	Y	N	N	Y	N	N	N	N	Y	N	Y	N	N
Trial	77	78	79	80	81	82	83	84	85	86	87	88	89
Results	N	N	N	N	Y	N	N	N	Y	Y	N	Y	N
Trial	90	91	92	93	94	95	96	97	98	99	100		
Results	Y	Y	N	N	Y	Y	Y	Y	N	Y	N		
Subtotal: 21 Yes, 29 No = 42%													
Total: 44 Yes, 56 No = 44%													

This experimental "resampling" estimation does not require a deck of cards. For example, one might create a 52-sided die, one side for each card in the deck, and roll it five times to get a "hand." But note one important part of the procedure: No single "card" is allowed to come up twice in the same set of five spins, just as no single card can turn up twice or more in the same hand. If the same "card" did turn up twice or more in a dice experiment, one could pretend that the roll had never taken place; this procedure is necessary to make the dice experiment analogous to the actual card-dealing situation under investigation. Otherwise, the results will be slightly in error. This type of sampling is known as "sampling without replacement," because each card is <u>not replaced</u> in the deck prior to dealing the next card (that is, prior to the end of the hand).

Still another resampling method uses a <u>random number table</u>, such as that which is shown in Table 4-2. Arbitrarily designate the spades as numbers 01-13, the diamonds as 14-26, the hearts as 27-39, and the clubs as 40-52. Then proceed across a row (or down a column), writing down each successive pair of digits, excluding pairs outside 01-52 and omitting duplication within sets of five numbers. Then translate them back into cards, and see how many "hands" of five "cards" contain one pair each. Table 4-3 shows six such hands, of which hands numbered 2, 3 and 6 contain pairs.

Table 4-2															
Table of Random Digits															
(see appendix for a longer table)															
48	52	78	38	11	90	41	83	43	99	51	55	57	03	83	20
15	11	84	33	09	24	08	52	42	70	37	16	66	73	15	54
25	89	70	11	91	65	41	90	88	04	30	72	15	81	34	46
34	24	66	55	67	79	29	18	36	56	96	95	35	06	05	10
37	27	58	38	23	84	94	39	99	50	74	80	41	85	98	63
12	17	04	68	19	98	53	44	16	32	91	01	71	60	19	12
88	85	44	65	52	01	99	56	72	07	96	39	56	34	86	01
81	92	77	83	10	58	92	33	63	48	62	66	32	61	59	74
08	50	15	18	13	45	65	12	32	92	53	82	07	61	71	80
84	29	90	36	05	95	20	71	17	82	83	38	01	87	74	92
77	76	46	28	47	15	04	21	04	75	51	83	91	37	14	32
01	33	90	94	86	10	03	99	95	98	76	97	97	26	45	62

Table 4-3
Six Simulated Trials for the Problem "OnePair"

	Aces	Deuces	3	4	5	6	7	8	9	10	Jack	Queen	King
Spades	01	02	03	04	05	06	07	08	09	10	11	12	13
Diamonds	14	15	16	17	18	19	20	21	22	23	24	25	26
Hearts	27	28	29	30	31	32	33	34	35	36	37	38	39
Clubs	40	41	42	43	44	45	46	47	48	49	50	51	52

Hand 1:	48	52	38	11	41	no pairs
Hand 2:	15	11	33	09	24	one pair
Hand 3:	25	11	41	04	30	one pair
Hand 4:	34	24	29	18	36	no pairs
Hand 5:	37	27	38	23	39	no pairs
Hand 6:	12	17	04	19	44	one pair

Now let's do the same job using RESAMPLING STATS on the computer. Let's call "One Pair" the file which simulates a deck of playing cards and solves the problem.

Our first task is to simulate a deck of playing cards analogous to the real cards we used previously. We don't need to simulate all the features of a deck, but only the features that matter for the problem at hand. We require a deck with four "1"s, four "2"s, etc., up to four "13"s. The suits don't matter for our present purposes. Therefore, with the CONCAT command (short for "concatenate" or join) we join together in a single array thirteen sets of numbers each from "1" to "4", to represent the 13 denominations.

At this point we have a complete deck in location A. But that "deck" is in the same order as a new deck of cards. If we do not shuffle the deck, the results will be predictable. Therefore, we write SHUFFLE A B and then deal a poker hand by taking the first five cards from the shuffled hand, using the TAKE statement. Now we must find out if there is one (and only one) pair; we do this with the MULTIPLES statement -- the "2" in that statement indicates that it is a duplicate, rather than a singleton or triplicate or quadruplicate that we are testing for -- and we put the result in location D. Next we SCORE in location Z how many pairs there are, the number in each trial being either zero, one, or two. And with that we end a single trial.

With the REPEAT 1000 statement and the END statement, we command the program to repeat a thousand times the statements in the "loop" between those two lines. When those 1000 repetitions are over, the computer moves on to COUNT the number of "1's" in SCOREkeeping vector Z, each "1" indicating a hand with a pair. And we then PRINT to the screen the result which is found in location K. If we want the <u>proportion</u> of the trials in which a pair occurs, we simply divide the results of the thousand trials by 1000.

Program "ONEPAIR"

```
CONCAT 4#1 4#2 4#3 4#4 4#5 4#6 4#7 4#8 4#9
4#10 4#11 4#12 4#13 A   Join together in an array (vector) four 1's,
                        four 2's, four 3's, etc., to represent a deck
                        of cards

REPEAT 1000             Repeat the following steps 1000 times

  SHUFFLE A B           Shuffle the deck

  TAKE B 1,5 C          Take the first five cards

  MULTIPLES C =2 D      How many pairs?

  SCORE D Z             Keep score of # of pairs

END                     End loop, go back and repeat

COUNT Z =1 K            How often 1 pair?

DIVIDE K 1000 KK        Convert to proportion

PRINT KK
```

In one run of the programs, KK was .419, so our estimate would be that the probability of a single pair is .419.

How accurate are these resampling estimates? The accuracy depends on the <u>number of hands</u> we deal -- the more hands, the greater

59

the accuracy. If we were to examine millions of hands, 42% would contain a pair each; that is, the chance of getting a pair in the long run is 42%. The estimate of 44 percent based on 100 hands in Table 4-1 is fairly close to the long-run estimate, though whether or not it is close enough depends on one's needs of course. If you need great accuracy, deal many more hands.

How many trials (hands) should be made for the estimate? There is no easy answer [1]. One approach is to run several (perhaps ten) equal sized sets of trials, and then examine whether the proportion of pairs found in the entire group of trials is very different from the proportions found in the various subgroup sets. If the proportions of pairs in the various subgroups differ greatly from one another or from the overall proportion, then keep running additional larger subgroups of trials until the variation from one subgroup to another is sufficiently small for your purposes. While such a procedure would be impractical using a deck of cards or any other physical means, it is relatively painless with the computer and RESAMPLING STATS.

ANOTHER INTRODUCTORY POKER PROBLEM

Which is more likely, poker hands with two pairs, or hands with three of a kind? This is a comparison problem, rather than a problem in absolute estimation as was the previous example.

In a series of 100 hands (using random numbers), four hands contained two pairs, and two hands contained three of a kind. Is it safe to say, on the basis of these 100 hands, that hands with two pairs are more frequent than hands with three of a kind? To check, we deal another 300 hands. Among them we see fifteen hands with two pairs (3.75 percent) and eight hands with three of a kind (2 percent), for a total of nineteen to ten. Although the difference is not enormous, it is reasonably clear-cut. Another 400 hands might be advisable, but we shall not bother.

Earlier we obtained forty-four hands with one pair each out of 100 hands, which makes it quite plain that one pair is more frequent than either two pairs or three-of-a-kind. Obviously, we need more hands to compare the odds in favor of two pairs with the odds in favor of three-of-a-kind than to compare those for one pair with those for either two pairs or three-of-a-kind. Why? Because the difference in odds between one pair, and either two pairs or three-of-a-kind, is much greater than the difference in odds between two pairs and three-of-a-kind. This observation leads to a general rule: The closer the odds between two events, the more trials are needed to determine which has the higher odds.

Again it is interesting to compare the odds with the mathematical computations, which are 1 in 21 (4.75 percent) for a hand containing two pairs and 1 in 47 (2.1 percent) for a hand containing three-of-a-kind -- not too far from the estimates of .0375 and .02 based on resampling.

To solve the problem with the aid of the computer, we simply need to estimate the proportion of hands having triplicates and the proportion of hands with two pairs, and compare those estimates.

To estimate the hands with three-of-a-kind, we can use a program just like "One Pair" earlier, except instructing the MULTIPLES statement to search for triplicates instead of duplicates. The program, then, is:

Program "3KIND"

```
CONCAT 4#1 4#2 4#3 4#4 4#5 4#6 4#7 4#8 4#9 4#10 4#11 4#12
4#13 A            Join together in an array (vector) called
                  "A" four 1's, four 2's, four 3's, etc., to
                  represent a deck of cards

REPEAT 1000       Repeat the following steps 1000 times

  SHUFFLE A B     Shuffle the deck

  TAKE B 1,5 C    Take the first five cards

  MULTIPLES C =3 D  How many triplicates?

  SCORE D Z       Keep score of # of pairs
```

```
END                    End loop, go back and repeat

COUNT Z =1 K           How often 1 pair?

DIVIDE K 1000 KK       Convert to proportion

PRINT KK
```

To estimate the probability of getting a two-pair, we revert to the original program (counting pairs), except that we examine all the results in SCOREkeeping vector Z for hands in which we had two pairs, instead of one.

Program "2PAIR"

```
CONCAT 4#1 4#2 4#3 4#4 4#5 4#6 4#7 4#8
4#9 4#10 4#11 4#12 4#13 A
                       Join together in an array (vector)
                       four 1's, four 2's, four 3's, etc.,
                       to represent a deck of cards

REPEAT 1000            Repeat the following steps 1000 times

  SHUFFLE A B          Shuffle the deck

  TAKE B 1,5 C         Take the first five cards

  MULTIPLES C =2 D     How many pairs?

  SCORE D Z            Keep score of # of pairs

END                    End loop, go back and repeat

COUNT Z =1 K           How often 1 pair?

DIVIDE K 1000 KK       Convert to proportion

PRINT KK
```

For efficiency (though efficiency really is not important here because the computer performs its operations so cheaply) we could develop both estimates in a single program by simply generating 1000 hands, and count the number with three-of-a-kind and the number with two pairs.

We have dealt with these first two examples in an intuitive, unsystematic fashion. From here on, however, we will work in an explicitly systematic step-by-step manner. And from here on the problems form an orderly sequence of the classical types of problems in probability theory (Chapter 4 and 5), and inferential statistics (Chapters 6 to 9).

SAMPLING FROM AN INFINITE UNIVERSE

Example 4-1: Three Daughters Among Four Children -- Two Outcome (Binomial [2]) Sampling with Equally Likely Outcomes; with Replacement

What is the probability that three of the four children in a four-child family will be daughters?

The first step is to state that the approximate probability that a single birth will produce a daughter is 50-50 (1 in 2). This estimate is not strictly correct, because there are roughly 106 male children born to each 100 female children. But the approximation is not too far off for most purposes, and the 50-50 split simplifies the job considerably. (Such "false" approximations are part of the everyday work of the scientist. The question is not whether or not a statement is "only" an approximation, but whether or not it is a good approximation for your purposes.)

The probability that a fair coin will turn up heads is .50 or 50-50, close to the probability of having a daughter. Therefore, flip a coin in groups of four flips, and count how often three of the flips produce heads. (You must decide in <u>advance</u> whether three heads means three girls or three boys.) It is as simple as that.

In resampling estimation it is of the highest importance to work in a careful, step-by-step fashion -- to write down the steps in the estimation, then to do the experiments just as described in the steps.

Here are a set of steps that will lead to a correct answer about the probability of getting three daughters among four children:

Step 1. Using coins, let "heads" equal "boy" and "tails" equal "girl."

Step 2. Throw four coins.

Step 3. Examine whether the four coins fall with exactly three tails up. If so, write "yes" on a record sheet; otherwise write "no."

Step 4. Repeat step 2 perhaps two hundred times.

Step 5. Count the proportion "yes." That proportion is an estimate of the probability of obtaining exactly 3 daughters in 4 children.

The first few experimental trials might appear in the record sheet as follows:

Number of Tails	Yes or No
1	No
0	No
3	Yes
2	No
1	No
2	No
.	.
.	.
.	.

The probability of getting three daughters in four births could also be found with a deck of cards, a random number table, a die, or with RESAMPLING STATS. For example, half the cards in a deck are black, so the probability of getting a black card ("daughter") from a full deck is 1 in 2. Therefore, deal a card, record "daughter" or "son," replace the card, shuffle, deal again, and so forth for 200 sets of four cards. Then count the proportion of groups of four cards in which you got four daughters.

A RESAMPLING STATS computer solution to the "3Girls" problem mimics the above steps:

Program "3GIRLS"

REPEAT 1000	Do 1000 trials
GENERATE 4 1,2 A	Generate 4 numbers at random, either 1 or 2. This is analogous to flipping a coin 4 times to generate 4 heads or tails. We keep these numbers in A, letting "1" represent girls.
COUNT A = 1 B	Count the number of girls and put the result in B.
SCORE B Z	Keep track of each trial result in Z.
END	End this trial, repeat the experiment until 1000 trials are complete, then proceed.
COUNT Z = 3 K	Count the number of experiments where we got exactly 3 girls, put this result in K.
DIVIDE K 1000 KK	Convert to a proportion.
PRINT KK	Print the results.

A note on the A's, B's, C's in the above program, etc.: These "variables" are called "vectors" in RESAMPLING STATS. A <u>vector</u> is an array of elements that is filled with different numbers as RESAMPLING STATS conducts its operations. When RESAMPLING STATS completes a trial, these vectors are generally wiped clean, except for the "SCORE" vector (here labeled "Z") which keeps track of the result of each trial.

To help keep things straight (though the program does not require it), we usually use "Z" to name the vector that collects all the trial results, and "K" to denote our overall summary results.

Notice that the procedure outlined in the steps above would have been different (though almost identical) if we asked about the probability of <u>three or more</u> daughters rather than <u>exactly three</u> daughters among four children. For <u>three or more</u> daughters we would have scored "yes" on our scorekeeping pad for either three or four heads, rather than for just three heads. Likewise, in the computer solution we would have used the command "Count Z >= 3 K."

It is important that, in this case, in contrast to what we did in Example 4-1, the introductory poker example, the card would be replaced each time so that each card is dealt from a full deck. This method is known as <u>sampling with replacement</u>. One samples with replacement whenever the successive events are <u>independent</u>; in this case we assume the chance of having a daughter remains the same (1 in 2) no matter what sex the previous births were. [3] But, if the first card dealt is black and is not replaced, the chance of the second card being black is no longer 26 in 52 (.50), but rather 25 in 51 (.49). If the first <u>three</u> cards are black and are not replaced, the chances of the fourth card's being black sink to 23 in 49 (.47).

To push the illustration further, consider what would happen if we used a deck of only six cards, half (3 of 6) black and half (3 of 6) red, instead of a deck of 52 cards. If the card were replaced each time, the 6-card deck would produce the same results as a 52-card deck; in fact, a two-card deck would do as well. But, if the sampling were done <u>without</u> replacement, it would be <u>impossible</u> to obtain 4 "daughters" with the 6-card deck because there are only 3 "daughters" in the deck.

66

To repeat, then, whenever you want to estimate the probability of some series of events where each event is independent of the other, you must sample with replacement.

A NOTE ON CLARIFYING AND LABELING PROBLEMS

In conventional texts and courses on analytic statistics, students are taught to distinguish between various classes of problems in order to decide which formula to apply. I doubt the wisdom of categorizing and labeling problems in that fashion. Rather, I consider it better that the student think through every new problem in the most fundamental terms. The exercise of doing so avoids the mistakes that come from too-hasty and superficial pigeon-holing of problems into categories. Nevertheless, in order that students who are studying analytic methods at the same time may be helped to connect up the resampling material with the conventional curriculum, the examples presented here are also described in conventional terms. And the examples given here cover the main sorts of problems encountered in probability and inferential statistics.

The problem of the 3 daughters is known in the conventional literature as a "binomial sampling experiment with equally-likely outcomes." "Binomial" means that the individual simple event (a birth or a coin flip) can have only two outcomes (boy or girl, heads or tails), "binomial" meaning "two names" in Latin [2].

A fundamental property of binomial processes is that the individual trials are independent, a concept discussed earlier. A binomial sampling process is a series of binomial events about which one may ask many sorts of questions -- the probability of exactly X heads ("successes") in N trials, or the probability of X or more "successes" in N trials, and so on.

"Equally likely outcomes" means we assume that the likelihood of a girl or boy in any one birth is the same (though this assumption is slightly contrary to fact) and we represent this with the equal likelihood heads and tails of a coin. Shortly we will come to binomial sampling experiments where the probability of the individual outcomes are not equal.

"With replacement" was explained earlier; if we were to use a red and black card deck (instead of a coin) for this resampling experiment, we would replace the card each time a card is drawn. Example 4-1, the introductory poker example, illustrated sampling without replacement, as will other examples to follow.

This problem would be done conventionally with the binomial theorem using probabilities of .5, asking about 3 successes in 4 trials.

Example 4-2: Three or More Successful Basketball Shots in Five Attempts (Two-Outcome Sampling with Unequally-Likely Outcomes, with Replacement -- A Binomial Experiment.)

What is the probability that a basketball player will score three or more baskets in five shots from a spot 30 feet from the basket, if on the average she succeeds with 25% of her shots from that spot?

In this case the probabilities of "success" or "failure" are not equal, in contrast to the previous problem of the daughters. Instead of a 50-50 coin, then, an appropriate "model" would be a thumbtack that has a 25% chance of landing "up" when it falls, and a 75% chance of landing down.

Lacking a thumbtack known to have a 25% chance of landing "up", we could use a card deck and let spades equal "success" and the other three suits represent "failure". Our resampling experiment could then be done as follows:

1. Let "spade" stand for "successful shot", and the other suits stand for unsuccessful shot.

2. Draw a card, record its suit and replace. Do so five times (for five shots).

3. Record whether the outcome of step 2 was three or more spades. If so indicate "yes", and otherwise "no".

4. Repeat steps 2-4 perhaps four hundred times.

5. Count the proportion "yes" out of the four hundred throws. That proportion estimates the probability of getting three or more baskets out of five shots if the probability of a single basket is .25.

The first three repetitions on your score sheet might look like this:

```
                   S  (Spade)              N
                   N  (Non-spade)          N
           1) No   N            2) No      N
                   N                       N
                   N                       N

                   N                       .
                   N                       .
          3) Yes   S                       .
                   S                       .
                   S                       .
```

Instead of cards, we could have used two-digit random numbers, with (say) "1-25" standing for "success," and "26-00" ("00" in place of "100") standing for failure. Then the steps would simply be:

1. Let the random numbers "1-25" stand for "successful shot," "26-00" for unsuccessful shot.

2. Draw five random numbers;

3. Count how many of the numbers are between "01" and "25." If three or more, score "yes."

4. Repeat step 2 four hundred times.

If you understand the earlier "Girls" program, then "Basketball" should be easy: To create 1000 samples, we start with a REPEAT statement. We then GENERATE 5 numbers between "1" and "4" to simulate the 5 shots, each with a 25 percent -- or 1 in 4 -- chance of scoring. We decide that "1" will stand for a successful shot, and "2" through "4" will stand for a missed shot, and therefore we COUNT the number of "1"'s in A to determine the number of shots resulting in baskets in the current sample. The next step is to transfer the results of each trial to vector Z by way of a SCORE statement. We then END the loop. The final step is to search the vector Z after the 1000 samples have been generated and COUNT the times that 3 or more baskets were made. We place the results in K, and then PRINT.

Program "BASKETBALL"

REPEAT 1000	Do 1000 experimental trials.
GENERATE 5 1,4 A	Generate 5 random numbers, each between 1 and 4, put them in A. Let "1" represent a basket, "2" through "4" be a miss.
COUNT A =1 B	Count the number of baskets, put them in B.
SCORE B Z	Keep track of each experiment's results in Z.
END	End the experiment, go back and repeat until all 1000 are completed, then proceed.
COUNT Z >= 3 K	Determine how many experiments produced more than two baskets, put that result in K.
DIVIDE K 1000 KK	Convert to a proportion.
PRINT KK	Print the result.

<u>Note to the Student of Analytic Probability Theory</u>: This problem would be done conventionally with the binomial theorem, asking about the chance of getting 3 successes in 5 trials, with the probability of a success = .25.

Example 4-3: Four Successful Shots in a Row -- The Multiplication Rule

---

Let us change the basketball facts a bit in order to learn a useful (though simple) bit of analytic probability theory. Assume that we want to know the probability of four successes in a row, instead of three or more successes out of five. The probability of a success on a given shot is still .25.

Instead of simulating the process with resampling trials we can, if we wish, arrive at the answer with what is known as the "Multiplication Rule". This rule says that the probability that <u>all</u> of a given number of <u>independent events</u> (the successful shots) will occur (four out of four in this case) is the <u>product</u> of their individual probabilities -- in this case, $1/4 \times 1/4 \times 1/4 \times 1/4 = 1/256$. If in doubt about whether the multiplication rule holds in any given case, however, you may check by resampling simulation. For the case of four daughters in a row, assuming that the probability of a girl is .5, the probability is $1/2 \times 1/2 \times 1/2 \times 1/2 = 1/16$.

An important point here, however: We have estimated the probability of a <u>particular</u> family having four daughters as 1 in 16 -- that is, odds of 15 to 1. But note: This is very different from stating that the odds are 15 to 1 against <u>some</u> family's having four daughters in a row. In fact, as many families will have four girls in a row as will have boy-girl-boy-girl in that order or girl-boy-girl-boy or <u>any other series</u> of four children. The chances against any particular series is the same -- 1 in 16 -- and one-sixteenth of all four-children families will have each of these series, on average. This means that if your next-door neighbor has four daughters, you cannot say "how out of the ordinary" the event is. It is easy to slip into unsound thinking about this matter.

71

Why do we multiply the probabilities of the independent simple events to learn the probability that they will occur jointly (the composite event)? Let us consider this in the context of three basketball shots each with 1/3 probability of hitting. In Figure 4-1, follow the dashed line first (- - -). One-third of the time the first shot will hit. Among that third of the first shots, a third will again hit on the second shot, that is, 1/3 of 1/3 or 1/3 x 1/3 = 1/9. The dashed line makes it clear that in 1/3 x 1/3 = 1/9 of the trials, two hits in a row will occur. Then, of the 1/9 of the total trials in which two hits in a row occur, 1/3 will go on to a third hit, or 1/3 x 1/3 x 1/3 = 1/27. Remember that we are dealing with independent events; regardless of whether the player made his first two shots, the probability is still 1 in 3 on the next shot.

Figure 4-1 is a tree diagram showing a set of sequential simple events where each event is conditional upon a prior simple event. Hence every probability after the first is a conditional probability.

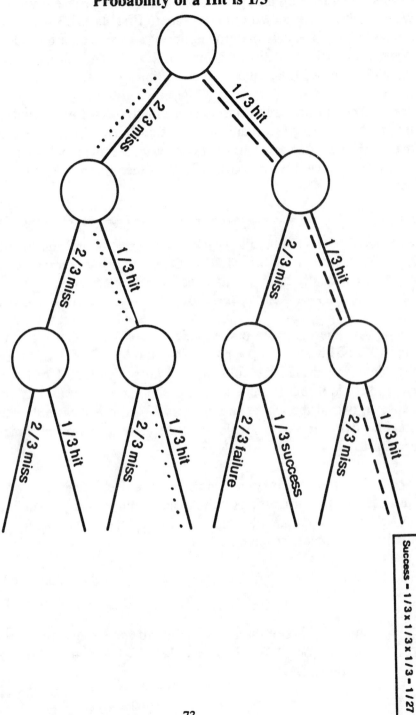

Figure 4-1
Tree Diagram for 3 Basketball Shots
Probability of a Hit is 1/3

Success = 1/3 x 1/3 x 1/3 = 1/27

Notice that the same rule gives us the probability of <u>any</u> <u>particular sequence</u> of hits and misses -- say, a miss then a hit then a hit -- which is traced by the dotted line (.......). The probability of a miss is 2/3. Among the trials with misses on the first shot, 1/3 will next have a hit, so 2/3 x 1/3 equals the probability of a miss then a hit. Of those trials, one third will then have a hit, or 2/3 x 1/3 x 1/3 = 2/27 equals the probability of the sequence miss-hit-hit.

The multiplication rule is exceedingly useful in every day life. It fits closely to a great many situations such as "What is the chance that it will rain (.3) and that (if it does rain) the plane will not fly (.8)?" Hence the probability of your not leaving the airport today is .3 x .8 = .24.

Example 4-4: One in the Black, Two in the White, and No Misses in Three Archery Shots (Multiple Outcome (Multinomial) Sampling With Unequally Likely Outcomes; with Replacement.)

Assume that from past experience you know that a given archer puts 10% of his shots in the black ("bullseye") and 60% of his shots in the white ring around the bullseye, and misses with 30% of his shots. How likely is it that in three shots the shooter will get exactly one bullseye, two in the white, and no misses? Notice that unlike the previous cases, in this example there are more than two outcomes for each trial.

This problem may be handled with a deck of three colors (or suits) of cards in proportions varying according to the probabilities of the various outcomes, and sampling with replacement. Using random numbers is simpler, however:

Step 1. Let "1" = "bullseye," "2-7" = "in the white," and "8-0" = "miss."

Step 2. Choose three random numbers, and examine whether there are one "1" and two numbers "2-7." If so, record "yes," otherwise "no."

Step 3. Repeat step 2 perhaps 400 times, and count the proportion of "yeses." This estimates the probability sought.

The first few shots might appear in the score sheet as follows:

Experimental Trial	# in Black	# in White	# Misses	Yes or No
1	0	2	1	No
2	2	0	1	No
3	0	3	0	No
4	1	2	0	Yes
5	1	0	2	No
6	0	2	1	No

This problem would be handled in conventional probability theory with what is known as the Multinomial Distribution.

This problem may be quickly solved on the computer with RESAMPLING STATS with the program labeled "Bullseye" below. Bullseye has a complication not found in previous problems. It tests whether two different sorts of events <u>both</u> happen, a bullseye plus two shots in the white.

After GENERATING three randomly-drawn numbers between 1 and 10, we check with the COUNT command to see if there is a bullseye. If there is, the IF statement tells the computer to continue with the operations, checking if there are two shots in the white; if there is no bullseye, the IF command tells the computer to END the trial and start another trial. A thousand repetitions are called for, the number of trials meeting the criteria are counted, and the results are then printed.

In addition to showing how this particular problem may be handled with RESAMPLING STATS, the Bullseye program teaches you some more fundamentals of computer programming. The IF statement, and the two loops, one within the other, are basic tools of programming.

Program "BULLSEYE"

REPEAT 1000 — Do 1000 experimental trials

GENERATE 3 1,10 A — To represent 3 shots, generate 3 numbers at random between 1 and 10 and put them in A. We will let a "1" denote a bullseye, "2" - "7" a shot in the white, and "8" - "10" a miss.

COUNT A =1 B — Count the number of bullseyes, put that result in B.

IF B = 1 — If there is exactly 1 bullseye, we will continue with counting the other shots. (If there are no bullseyes, we need not bother -- the outcome we are interested in has not occurred.)

COUNT A between 2 7 C — Count the number of shots in the white, put them in C. (Recall we are doing this only if we got 1 bullseye.)

SCORE C Z — Keep track of the results of this second count.

END — End the "IF" sequence -- we will do the following steps without regard to the "IF" condition.

END — End the above experiment and repeat it until 1000 repetitions are complete, then continue.

COUNT Z =2 K — Count the number of occasions on which there are two in the white and a bullseye.

DIVIDE K 1000 KK   Convert to a proportion.

PRINT KK   Print the results.

Perhaps the logic would be clearer if we added statements that IF B = 0 (that is, no bullseye), a zero is put into the SCORE vector. Then the SCORE vector would contain an entry for each trial. But adding these statements would lengthen the program and therefore make it seem more complex. Hence they are omitted.

THE ADDITION RULE

This is a good place to present a second fundamental rule of analytic statistics, the "Addition Rule." In Example 4-4, a bullseye, an in-the-white shot, and a missed shot are "mutually exclusive" events because a single shot cannot result in more than one of the three possible outcomes. One can calculate the probability of <u>either of two</u> mutually-exclusive outcomes by adding their probabilities. The probability of <u>either</u> a bullseye or a shot in the white is .1 + .6 = .7. The probability of an arrow <u>either</u> in the white <u>or</u> a miss is .6 + .3 = .9. The logic of the Addition Rule is obvious when we examine the random numbers given to the outcomes. Seven of 10 random numbers belong to "bullseye" or "in the white," and nine of 10 belong to "in the white" or "miss."

More generally, one can calculate the probability of one among a set of mutually-exclusive alternatives by adding their probabilities. The simple Addition Rule often comes in handy.

Example 4-5: Eight or More Points in Seven Shots

If the archer in Example 4-4 gets three points for a bullseye and one point for being in the white, and if her probabilities are as in Example 4-4, what is the chance of getting eight or more points in seven shots?

This is a second sort of question that one may ask of multiple-outcome situations with replacement. The solution would be rather difficult with conventional methods, but the resampling approach is fast and easy, as the following program "Archery" illustrates:

Program "ARCHERY"

REPEAT 1000	Do 1000 experimental trials.
GENERATE 7 1,10 A	Generate 7 shots between 1 and 10, the same as in the previous example.
COUNT A =1 B	Count the number of bullseyes; put the result in B.
MULTIPLY B 3 C	Multiply that number by 3 (3 points for each bullseye) and put the result in C.
COUNT A between 2 7 D	Count the number of shots in the white; put the result in D. Since each of the white shots counts as 1 point, we need not multiply them by anything.
ADD C D E	Add up the total points, put the result in E.
SCORE E Z	Keep score of each experiment's total points in Z.
END	End the loop for one experiment (trial); go back and keep repeating until all 1000 are complete, then proceed.

COUNT Z > 7 K	Determine how many experiments produced more than 7 points, record the result in K.
DIVIDE K 1000 KK	Convert to a proportion.
HISTOGRAM Z	Graph the results of all the trials.
PRINT K	Print the summary result -- the number of trials where we got more than 7 points.

Graphing the results of all the trials yields a histogram. The possible point totals are listed along the X-axis, while the Y-axis denotes the frequency with which those point totals occurred in our 1000 trials.

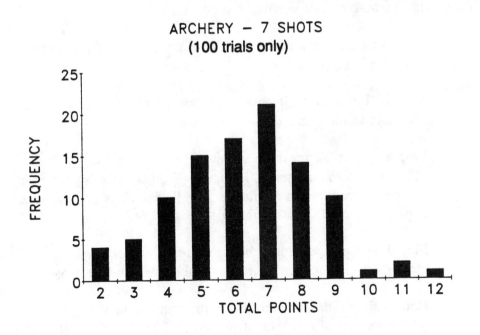

ARCHERY – 7 SHOTS
(100 trials only)

Example 4-6: The Birthday Problem (The Probability of Duplication in a Multi-Outcome Sample from an Infinite Universe) (File "Birthday)

As an indication of the power <u>and</u> simplicity of resampling methods, consider this famous examination question used in probability courses: What is the probability that two or more people among a roomful of, say, twenty-five people will have the same birthday? To answer, we may simply examine the first twenty-five numbers from the random-number table that fall between "001" and "365" (the number of days in the year), record whether or not there is a duplication among the twenty-five, and repeat the process often enough to obtain a reasonably stable probability estimate.

Pose the question to a mathematical friend of yours, watch her or him sweat for a while, and compare your answer to hers/his. (I think you will find the correct answer very surprising. People who know how this problem works have been known to take advantage of this knowledge by making and winning big bets on it.)

More specifically, these steps answer the question for the case of twenty-five people in the room:

Step 1. Let three-digit random numbers "001-365" stand for the 365 days in the year. (Ignore leap year for simplicity.)

Step 2. Examine for duplication among the first twenty-five random numbers chosen "001-365". (Triplicates or higher-order repeats are counted as duplicates here.) If there is one or more duplicate, record "yes." Otherwise record "no."

Step 3. Repeat perhaps a thousand times, and calculate the proportion of a duplicate birthday among twenty-five people.

Here is the first experiment from a random-number table, starting at the top left of the page of numbers: 021, 158, 116, 066, 353, 164, 019, 080, 312, 020, 353...

Handling the "Birthday" problem with RESAMPLING STATS is amazingly simple. First, GENERATE 25 numbers between "1" and "365" into A. Then, to determine whether any two people have the same birthday, the MULTIPLES statement checks whether the same number came up more than once. Next, SCORE this result from B into Z. REPEAT, say, 1000 times. After the END of the loop, COUNT in Z the number of samples out of the 1000 trials that had at least one birthday shared by two or more people. This result is placed in K.

Now try the program -- you may be surprised at the result.

Program "BIRTHDAY"

REPEAT 1000	Do 1000 trials (experiments)
GENERATE 25 1,365 A	Generate 25 numbers randomly between 1 and 365, put them in A.
MULTIPLES A > 1 B	Looking in A, count the number of multiples and put the result in B. We request multiples > 1 because we are interested in any multiple, whether it is a duplicate, triplicate, etc. Had we been interested only in duplicates, we would have put in MULTIPLES A = 2 B.
SCORE B Z	Score the result of each trial to Z.
END	End the loop for the trial, go back and repeat the trial until all 1000 are complete, then proceed.
COUNT Z > 0 K	Determine how many trials had at least one multiple.
DIVIDE K 1000 KK	Convert to a proportion.
PRINT KK	Print the result.

The next two problems are a bit harder than the previous ones, and you might skip them for now but come back to them later.

Two players, each with a stake of ten pennies, engage in the following game: A coin is tossed, and if it is (say) heads, player A must give player B a penny; if it is tails, player B must give player A a penny. What is the probability that one player will lose his or her entire stake of 10 pennies if they play for 200 tosses?

This is a classic problem in probability theory which has many everyday applications in situations such as inventory management. For example, what is the likelihood of going out of stock of a given item in a given week if customers and deliveries arrive randomly?

Solution of the penny-matching problem with coins is straightforward. Repeatedly flip a coin and check if one player or the other reaches a zero balance before you reach 200 flips. Or with random numbers:

Step 1. Numbers "1-5" = head = "+1"; Numbers "6-0" = tail = "-1".

Step 2. Proceed down a series of 200 numbers, keeping a running tally of the "+1"'s and the "-1"'s. If the tally reaches "+10" or "-10" on or before the two-hundredth digit, record "yes"; otherwise record "no".

Step 3. Repeat step 2 perhaps 400 or 1000 times, and calculate the proportion of "yeses". This estimates the probability sought.

The following RESAMPLING STATS program will also solve the problem -- follow along in its logic. You will find it easier if you start out at the sixth line where the program models a coin flip with the STATEMENT "GENERATE 1 1,2 C." Then go on to identify the REPEAT 200 loop that describes the procedure for flipping a coin 200 times. Finally, note how the REPEAT 1000 loop simulates 1000 games, each game consisting of 200 coin flips.

Program "PENNIES"

REPEAT 1000	Do 1000 trials
NUMBERS (10) A	Record the number 10: A's stake
NUMBERS (10) B	Same for B
NUMBERS (0) flag	An indicator flag that will be set to "1" when somebody wins
REPEAT 200	Repeat the following steps 200 times
GENERATE 1 1,2 C	Generate the equivalent of a coin flip, letting 1 = heads, 2 = tails
IF C =1	If it's a heads
ADD B 1 B	Add 1 to B's stake
SUBTRACT A 1 A	Subtract 1 from A's stake
END	End the IF condition
IF C = 2	If it's a tails
ADD A 1 A	Add one to A's stake
SUBTRACT B 1 B	Subtract 1 from B's stake
END	End the IF condition
IF A = 20	If A has won
COPY (1) flag	Set the indicator flag to 1
END	End the IF condition
IF B = 20	If B has won

COPY (1) flag	Set the indicator flag to 1
END	End the If condition
END	End the repeat loop for 200 plays (note that the indicator flag stays at 0 if neither A nor B has won)
SCORE flag Z	Keep track of whether anybody won
END	End the 1000 trials
COUNT Z =1 K	Find out how often somebody won
DIVIDE K 1000 KK	Convert to a proportion
PRINT KK	PRINT the results

A similar example: A warehouse starts out with a supply of twelve capacirators. Every three days a new shipment of two capacirators is received. There is a .6 probability that a capacinator will be used each morning, and the same each afternoon. (That is, it is as if a random drawing is made each half-day to see if a capacirator is used; two capacirators may be used in a single day, or one or none). How long will be it, on the average before the warehouse runs out of stock?

Example 4-7: A Drunk's Random Walk

If a drunk chooses the direction of each step randomly, will he ever get home? If he can only walk on the road on which he lives the problem is almost the same as the gambler's ruin problem above ("Pennies"). But if the drunk can go in more than two directions, then the problem becomes a bit different and interesting.

Looking now at Figure 4-2, what is the probability of the drunk reaching either his house (at 3 steps east, 2 steps north) or my house (1 west, 4 south) before he finishes taking twelve steps?

One way to handle the problem would be to use a four-directional spinner such as is used with a child's board game, and then keep track of each step on a piece of graph paper. The reader may construct a RESAMPLING STATS program as an exercise.

Figure 4-2

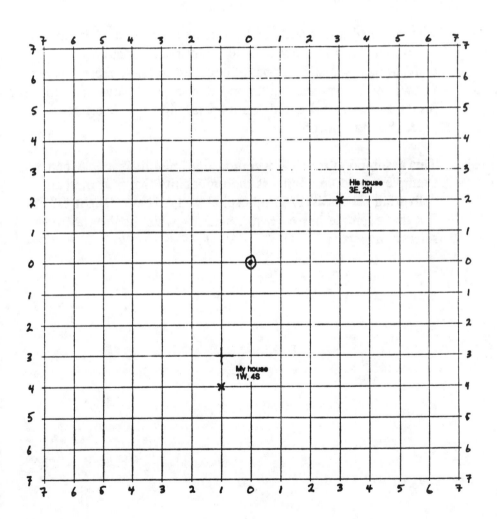

NOTES:

[1] One simple rule-of-thumb is to quadruple the original number. The reason for quadrupling is that _four_ times as big a sample gives _twice_ as much accuracy (as measured by the standard deviation, the most frequent measurement of accuracy). That is, the error decreases with the square root of the sample size. If you see that you need _much_ more accuracy, then _immediately_ increase the sample size even more than four times - perhaps ten or a hundred times.

[2] Conventional labels such as "binomial" are used here for general background and as guideposts to orient the student of conventional statistics. You do not need to know these labels to understand the resampling approach; one of the advantages of resampling is that it avoids errors resulting from incorrect pigeonholing of problems.

[3] This assumption is slightly contrary to scientific fact. A better example would be: What is the probability that four mothers delivering successively in a hospital will all have daughters? But that example has other difficulties - which is the way science always is.

CHAPTER 5

SAMPLING FROM FINITE UNIVERSES: PROBABILITY THEORY, PART 2

INTRODUCTION

The difference between this chapter and Chapter 4 is that this one deals with problems in which you sample without replacement. In such cases, it is important to remember that the single events are no longer independent. A typical situation in which sampling without replacement occurs is when items are chosen from a finite universe -- for example, when children are selected randomly from a classroom. If the class has five boys and five girls, and if you were to choose three girls in a row, then the chance of selecting a fourth girl on the next choice is lower than the chance that you would pick a girl on the first selection.

The key to solving this type of problem is the same as with earlier problems: you must choose a simulation procedure which produces simple events having the same probabilities as the simple events in the actual problem involving sampling without replacement. That is, you must make sure that your simulation does not allow duplication of events that have already occurred. The easiest way to sample without replacement with resampling techniques is by simply ignoring an outcome if it has already occurred.

The examples in Chapter 4 (except for the introductory poker examples) dealt with infinite universes, in which the probability of a given simple event is unaffected by the outcome of the previous simple event. But now we move on to finite universes, situations in which you begin with a given set of objects whose number is not enormous -- say, a total of two, or two hundred, or two thousand. If we liken such a ' situation to an urn containing balls of different colors each with a number on it, we are interested in the likelihood of drawing various sets of numbered and colored balls from the urn on the condition that we do not replace balls after they are drawn.

This chapter also describes the general procedure used in solving problems in probability and statistics with the resampling method. It sets down the steps that one follows in simulating a universe of interest in such fashion that one may, by random drawings, deduce the probability of various events. Having had the experience of working through the problems in Chapter 3 and the beginning of Chapter 4, the reader should now have a solid basis to follow the description of the general procedure, which will then help in dealing with specific problems.

Examples 5-1 through 5-6 deal with some of the more important sorts of questions one may ask about drawings without replacement from such an urn. To get an overview, I suggest that you read over the titles of Examples 5-1 to 5-6 before beginning to work through the examples themselves.

Let us begin by describing some of the major sorts of problems with the aid of an urn with six balls.

Case 1. Each of the six balls is labeled with a number between "1" and "6". We ask: What is the probability of choosing balls 1, 2, and 3 in that order if we choose three balls without replacement? Figure 5-1 diagrams the events we consider "success".

Figure 5-1
The Event Classified as "Success" for the Problem (File "Inorder")

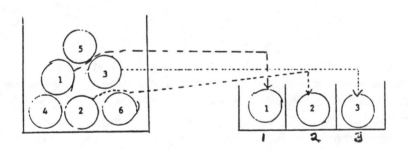

Case 2. We begin with the same urn, but now ask the probability of choosing balls 1, 2, and 3 in any order if we choose three balls without replacement. Figure 5-2 diagrams two of the events we consider success. These possibilities include that which is shown in Figure 5-1 above, plus other possibilities.

Figure 5-2
An Incomplete List of the Events Classified as "
Success for Case 2 (File "Anyorder")

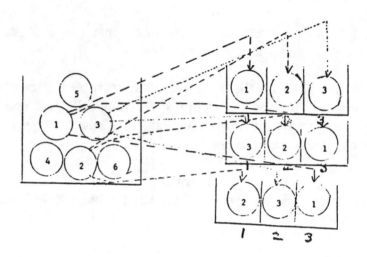

Case 3. The odd-numbered balls are painted red and the even-numbered balls are painted black. What is the probability of getting a red ball and then a black ball in that order? Some of the possibilities are illustrated in Figure 5-3, which includes the possibility shown in Figure 5-1. It also includes <u>some but not</u> all possibilities found in Figure 5-2; for example, Figure 5-2 includes choosing balls 2, 3 and 1 in that order, but Figure 5-3 does not.

Figure 5-3
An Incomplete List of the Events Classified as "Success" for Case 3 (File "Oddeven")

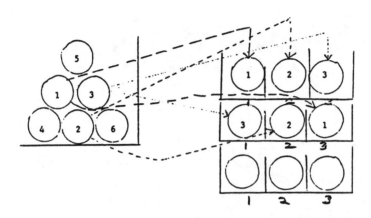

Case 4. What is the probability of getting two red balls and one black ball in any order?

Figure 5-4
An Incomplete List of the Events Classified as " Success" for Case 4 (File "Tworeds")

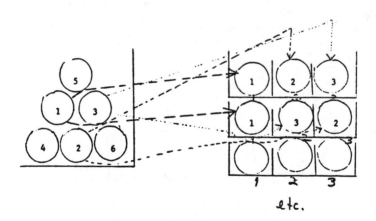

etc.

Case 5. Various questions about <u>matching</u> may be asked. For example, what is the probability of getting ball 1 on the first draw <u>or</u> ball 2 on the second draw <u>or</u> ball 3 on the third draw? (Figure 5-5) Or, what is the probability of getting all balls on the draws corresponding to their numbers?

Figure 5-5
An Incomplete List of the Events Classified as
"Success for Case 5 (File "Onematch")

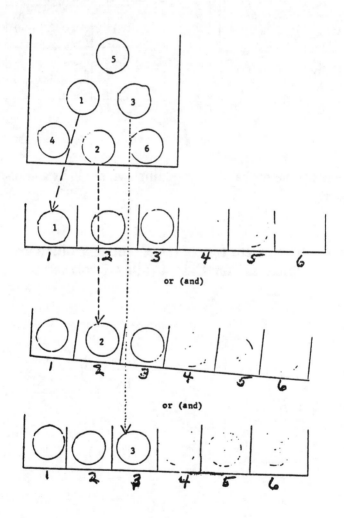

Example 5-1: What is the Probability of Selecting Four Girls and One Boy When Selecting Five Students From Any Twenty-five Girls and Twenty-five Boys? (Sampling Without Replacement When There are Two Outcomes and the Order Does Not Matter)

The important difference between this example and examples in the prior chapter is that the probability of obtaining a boy or a girl in a single simple event <u>differs</u> from one event to the next in this example. To illustrate, the probability of a girl is .5 (25 out of 50) when the first student is chosen, but the probability of a girl is either 25/49 or 24/49 when the second student is chosen, depending on whether a boy or a girl was chosen on the first pick. Or after, say, three girls and one boy are picked, the probability of getting a girl on the next choice is (25-3)/(50-4) = 22/46 which is clearly not equal to .5.

As always, we must create a satisfactory analog to the process whose probability we want to learn. In this case, we can use a deck of 50 cards, half red and half black, and deal out five cards <u>without replacing them</u> after each card is dealt; this simulates the choice of five students from among the fifty.

We can also work the example with random numbers. But if so, we cannot simply designate "01-25" as boys and "26-50" as girls (ignoring 51-00 when they occur), because if we did so the probability of a girl would be the same on each pick. Instead, to simulate non-replacement, we specify that no number can be taken into the sample twice, just as no student can be chosen twice. That is, if we come across a number more than once, we simply ignore it after the first occurrence. More specifically:

Step 1. Let "01-25" = girls, "26-50" = boys

Step 2. Select five non-duplicating numbers; if a number comes up more than once, ignore it. Count whether there are four numbers "01-25", and one "26-50". If so, write "yes", otherwise "no".

Step 3. Repeat step 2 perhaps 400 times, and count the proportion "yes", which estimates the probability sought.

Here are the results of a few experimental trials:

Experiment	Numbers Chosen	Success ?
1	18, 22, [18 selected but ignored] 27, 2, 49	No
2	37, 19, 18, 7, 9	Yes
3	13, 14, 2, 29, 24	Yes
.		
.		
.		

It is important to notice that in this problem we do not distinguish among particular girls (or boys). That is, it does not matter which girl (or boy) is selected in a given trial. Nor did we pay attention to the order in which we selected girls or boys. This is an instance of Case 4 discussed above. Subsequent problems will deal with situations where the order of selection, and the particular individuals, do matter.

A solution to this problem with RESAMPLING STATS is presented below. Let's go through the steps.

We ask the probability of randomly selecting four girls out of five children in a classroom of fifty children with equal numbers of boys and girls. We simulate the class by creating an array A with numbers "1" through "50" in order, designating "1" through "25" as girls and "26" through "50" boys. We then REPEAT the following steps a thousand times.

We first SHUFFLE the elements of Vector A into Vector B to randomize the order of the children. We next TAKE the first five children in this randomly-ordered array B and place them in C. This simulates the random selection of five children. Then we COUNT the number of girls--numbers "1" to "25"--in C. Next, we SCORE the number of girls selected for each random sample into D. We need not concern ourselves with whether one boy was chosen, because we know that if four (and only four) girls are chosen, one boy must have been selected as well.

After the thousand samples are completed, we determine how many of the random samples of five children contained four girls by COUNTing the number of times four girls were selected. Finally, we PRINT the result.

Program "FOURGIRL"

NUMBERS 1,50 A	Constitute the set of girls (numbers 1-25) and boys (26-50) and put those numbers in A.
REPEAT 1000	Repeat the following steps 1000 times.
SHUFFLE A B	Shuffle the numbers, call the shuffled vector B.
TAKE B 1,5 C	Take the first 5 numbers, call them C.
COUNT C between 1 25 D	Count how many girls (numbers 1-25) there are, put the result in D.
SCORE D Z	Keep track of each trial result in Z.
END	End the experiment, go back and repeat until all 1000 trials are complete.
COUNT Z =4 K	Count the number of times we got four girls, put the result in K.

95

DIVIDE K 1000 KK	Convert to a proportion.
PRINT KK	Print the result.

We can also find the probabilities of other outcomes from a histogram of trial results obtained with the following command:

HISTOGRAM Z	Produce a histogram of trial results.

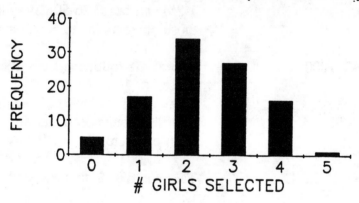

From this histogram, we can see that in 16% of the trials, 4 of the 5 selected were girls.

It should be noted that for this problem -- as for most other problems -- there are several other resampling procedures that will also do the job correctly.

In analytic probability theory this problem is worked with a formula for "combinations".

This problem is similar to Example 5-1 except that now there are four equally-likely outcomes instead of only two. The RESAMPLING STATS solution is straightforward in the program "9spades."

Program "9SPADES"

NUMBERS 1,52 A	Constitute the deck of 52 cards, numbers 1-52 in vector A. We will let 1-13 = spades, 14-26 = clubs, etc.
REPEAT 1000	Repeat the trial 1000 times.
SHUFFLE A B	Shuffle the deck, call the shuffled deck B.
TAKE B 1,13 C	Deal out one hand of 13 cards. (Take the first 13 numbers from B and call them C.
COUNT C between 1 13 D	Count the number of spades in C, put the result in D.
IF D = 9	If we have nine spades, we'll continue on to count the clubs. If we don't have nine spades, the number of clubs is irrelevant --we have not gotten the hand we are interested in.

COUNT C between 14 26 E	Count the clubs, put the result in E.
SCORE E Z	Keep track of the number of clubs in each experiment in Z.
END	End the IF condition.
END	End the experiment, go back and repeat all 1000 trials (experiments) are complete.
COUNT Z =4 K	Count the number of trials where we got 4 clubs. This is the answer we want --the number of hands out of 1000 with 9 spades and 4 clubs. (Recall that we only counted the clubs if the hand already had 9 spades.)
DIVIDE K 1000 KK	Convert to a proportion.
PRINT KK	

This problem bears the same relationship to Example 5-2 that Example 4-5 bears to Example 4-4.

Program "BRIDGE"

NUMBERS (1 1 1 1 2 2 2 2 3 3 3 3 4 4 4 4) A

> Constitute the set A of face cards, with numbers corresponding to their point value (i.e. 4 jacks, 4 queens, 4 kings, 4 aces)

SET 36 0 B

> Constitute a set of 36 0's to represent the rest of the deck, which does not score points.

CONCAT A B C

> Put the deck together.

REPEAT 1000

> Do 1000 trials.

SHUFFLE C D

> Shuffle the deck of cards.

TAKE D 1,13 E

> Take thirteen cards.

SUM E G

> Total the points.

SCORE G Z

> Keep score of the result.

END

> End one experiment, go back and repeat until all 1000 are done.

HISTOGRAM Z

> Produce a histogram of trial results.

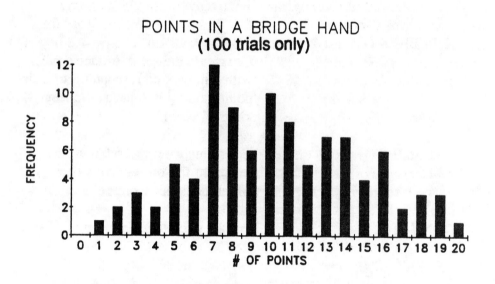

POINTS IN A BRIDGE HAND
(100 trials only)

From this histogram, we see that in 4% of our trials, we obtained a total of exactly 15 points. RESAMPLING STATS will calculate this for us directly if we add the following commands on to the program:

COUNT Z = 15 K   How many times did we have a hand with fifteen points?

DIVIDE K 1000 KK   Convert to a proportion.

PRINT KK   Print the result.

Example 5-4: Four Girls and Then One Boy From Twenty-five Girls and Twenty-five Boys (Order Matters, Sampling Without Replacement, Two Outcomes, Several of Each Item)

What is the probability of getting an ordered series of four girls and then one boy, from a universe of twenty-five girls and twenty-five boys? This illustrates Case 3 above. Clearly we can use the same sampling mechanism as in Example 5-1, but now we record "yes" for a smaller number of composite events. We record "no" if only one boy is chosen but he is chosen 1st, 2nd, 3rd, or 4th, whereas in Example 5-1 such outcomes are recorded "yes".

Step 1. Let "01-25" = girls, "26-50" = boys.

Step 2. Select five non-duplicating numbers. Check whether the series includes four numbers "01-25" followed by a number "26-50". If so, write "yes", otherwise "no".

Step 3. Repeat step 2 perhaps 1000 times, and count the proportion "yes" which estimates the probability sought.

The RESAMPLING STATS program "4girlboy" starts out similarly to the earlier problem "Fourgirls." As in that problem, an array simulating a class of 50 children is created. But whereas in the previous problem any 4 of the first 5 children had to be girls, in this problem, the first 4 children must be girls, and then the fifth must be a boy for a trial to be considered a success. We thus TAKE the first 4 randomly-chosen children and place them in C. We must then determine the number of these children which are girls by counting those that have a number between "1" and "25", and placing the result in D.

If we find that all 4 of the children selected are girls, then we proceed to pick a fifth child and put it in E. If, however, of the first 4 children selected all were not girls, then we skip the steps through the first END statement, because we would already know that this trial will not be a "success." To determine whether this fifth child selected is a boy -- that is, checking whether it has a number between "26" and "50" -- we use a COUNT statement. If it is a boy, then F will equal "1"; if it is not a boy, then F will equal "0". (Remember that if the first 4 children selected were not all girls, then F will not get any value.) We then SCORE the value in F to E. This ends the conditional statement and the loop.

Program "4GIRLBOY"

NUMBERS 1,50 A	Constitute the set of girls (numbers 1-25) and boys (numbers 26-50), put them in A.
REPEAT 1000	Do the following experimental trial 1000 times.
SHUFFLE A B	Shuffle the numbers, put the shuffled numbers in B.
TAKE B 1,4 C	Take the first 4 numbers, put them in C.
COUNT C between 1 25 D	Count the number of girls, put the result in D.
IF D = 4	If we have 4 girls...
TAKE B 5 E	Take the fifth number (not 5 numbers) from B and put it in E.
COUNT E between 26 50 F	How many boys in E? (It would have to be either 0 or 1.
SCORE F Z	Keep track of each trial result.
END	End the IF condition

END	End the experiment, go back and repeat until all 1000 are complete.
COUNT Z =1 K	Count the number of trials in which we got 1 boy (recall that we only counted the boy if we had already gotten the required 4 girls.)
DIVIDE K 1000 KK	Convert to a proportion.
PRINT KK	Print the result.

This type of problem is conventionally done with a "permutation" formula.

THE GENERAL PROCEDURE

Until now, the steps to follow in solving particular problems have been chosen to fit the specific facts of that problem. And so they must. But we can also describe the steps more generally. The generalized procedure describes what we are doing when we estimate a probability using resampling problem-solving operations. (The general steps are designated by letters rather than numbers here, because more than one step in a particular resampling experiment may be necessary to complete a general step described here. The steps will later be described in greater detail when we consider situations in which the universe in which we are interested has unknown characteristics.

STEP A. Construct a universe of random numbers or cards or dice or some other randomizing mechanism that has a composition similar to the universe whose behavior we wish to simulate and describe. Universe refers to the system that is relevant for a single simple event. For example:

a) A coin with two sides, or two sets of random numbers "1-5" and "6-0," simulates the system that produces a single male or female birth, when we are estimating the probability of three girls in the first four children. Notice that in this universe the probability of a girl remains the same from trial event to trial event -- that is, the events are independent -- demonstrating a universe from which we sample with replacement.

b) A deck of 25 red and 25 black cards simulates a group of 25 boys and 25 girls from which we draw a sample of five students.

Hard thinking is required in order to determine the appropriate "real" universe whose properties interest you. Once the choice of universe is made, however, it is relatively easy to choose the appropriate simulation model.

STEP(S) B. Specify the procedure that produces a sample which simulates the real-life sample we are interested in. That is, you must indicate the procedural rules by which the sample is drawn from the simulated universe. These rules must correspond to the behavior of the real universe in which you are interested. To put it another way, the simulation procedure must produce simple experimental events with the same probabilities that the simple events have in the real world. For example:

a) In the case of three daughters in four children, the procedure is to draw a card and then replace it if you are using cards. If you are using a random-numbers table, the random numbers automatically simulate replacement. Just as the chances of having a boy or a girl do not change depending on the sex of the preceding child, so we want to ensure through replacement that the chances do not change each time we choose from the deck of cards.

b) In the case of the five students chosen from among 25 boys and 25 girls, the procedure is to ignore duplicate numbers if you use random numbers "1-25" and "26-50", so as to simulate non-replacement.

Recording the outcome of the sampling must be indicated as part of this step, e.g. "record 'yes' if girl, 'no' if boy."

STEP(S) C. If several simple events must be combined into a composite event, and if the composite event was not described in the procedure in step B, describe it now. For example:

a) For the three girls in four children, the procedure for each simple event of a single birth was described in step B. Now we must specify repeating the simple events four times.

b) In the case of the five students from the class of 25 boys and 25 girls, the entire sampling procedure was described in step B, so no further step corresponding to step C is needed.

Recording of "yes" or "no," "success" or "failure," is part of this step. This records the results of all the independent trials and is the basis for a tabulation of the final result.

STEP(S) D. Calculate from the tabulation of outcomes of the resampling trials the proportion of "yes" or "no," "success" or "failure" that estimates the probability we wish to estimate in step C.

There is indeed more than one way to skin a cat (ugh!). And there is always more than one way to correctly estimate a given probability. Therefore, when reading through the list of steps set forth here to estimate a given probability, please keep in mind that a particular list is not sacred or unique; other sets of steps will also do the trick.

Example 5-5: Four or More Couples Getting Their Own Partners When Ten Couples are Paired Randomly (Probability of Matching by Chance) (Program "Couples")

Ten couples of boys and girls come to a party. In order to get them acquainted with each other, the host pairs them at random for the first dance by picking a boy's name from one hat and a girl's name from another. What is the chance that four or more couples will get the partners they came with?

By now the solution seems obvious to you: Simulate the drawings from the two hats filled with boys' and girls' names, and see how often four or more matches occur.

Step 1. Let "ace" through "10" of hearts be girls, "ace" through "10" of spades be boys.

Step 2. Shuffle the hearts and deal them out in a row; shuffle the spades and deal in a row just below the hearts.

Step 3. Count the pairs -- a pair is one card from the heart row and one card from the spade row -- that contain the same denomination. If 4 or more pairs match, record "yes," otherwise "no."

Step 4. Repeat steps (2) and (3) perhaps 200 times.

Step 5. Count the proportion "yes." This estimates the probability of 4 or more pairs.

Exercise for the student: write the steps to do this example with random numbers.

Now let's examine the RESAMPLING STATS solution "Couples". The key step is to fill array A with 10 elements numbered "1" to "10" in order, with each number standing for a male. We fill array B in similar fashion to represent the females.

In each of the 1000 samples we SHUFFLE the elements of B, which stands for the females, to create a new vector C. As long as either the males or the females are randomly ordered, the probability of getting a correct match is determined by chance. There are several ways to determine whether a match occurs. Our method is using the SUBTRACT command to compare each element of A with each element of C. A match causes a "0", this would mean that the third couple was matched correctly because they have the same numbers -- "3"s. We then COUNT the number of "0"s in D to determine the number of couples correctly matched in the current sample. The result for the current sample is placed in E, then transferred to Z in order to keep SCORE for each of the 1000 samples. This ends the loop.

Program "COUPLES"

NUMBERS 1,10 A	An array of 10 males.
NUMBERS 1,10 B	An identical array of 10 females -- the pair for each of the males.
REPEAT 1000	Do the experiment 1000 times.
SHUFFLE B C	Shuffle the females.
SUBTRACT A C D	This operation pairs each shuffled female with a male and subtracts. If it is an original pairing (1/1, 2/2, etc.), the result will be a 0. The number of 0's indicates how many of the 10 males got paired up again with their original partner.
COUNT D =0 E	Count the number of 0's and put the result in E.
SCORE E Z	Keep track of each trial result.
END	End the trial, go back and repeat until all 1000 are complete.
HISTOGRAM Z	Produce a histogram of the results.

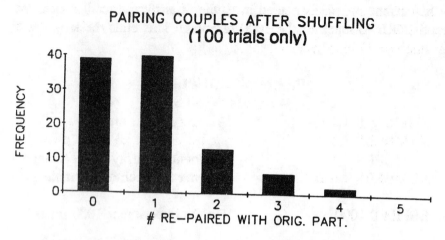

PAIRING COUPLES AFTER SHUFFLING
(100 trials only)

FREQUENCY

RE-PAIRED WITH ORIG. PART.

From this histogram, we see that in only 3% of the trials did 4 or more couples end up being re-paired with their own partners. We can calculate this proportion directly with RESAMPLING STATS:

COUNT Z >= 4 K   Determine how many trials had 4 or more males being matched with their partner after the shuffling. (Note that this is the same as the number of females being matched with their original partner.)

DIVIDE K 1000 KK   Convert to a proportion.

PRINT KK   Print the result.

Another famous problem of this sort: The hat-checker at a restaurant mixes up the hats of a party of 6 men. What is the probability that at least one will get his own hat?

Instead of matching men with women, as in the earlier problem, however, we are now matching men with their hats. See the program "Hats" for the solution. First, assign each of the 6 men a number, and place these numbers in A. Next, assign each man's hat the same number in B, but arrange them in random order by shuffling the numbers from B into C, which represents the group of mixed-up hats.

The rest of the problem is the same as in "Couples" except that in the second COUNT statement, we now are interested in any trial where at least one (>= 1) man received the right hat.

Program "HATS"

NUMBERS 1,6 A	Constitute the set of six men.
NUMBERS 1,6 B	Constitute the set of their six hats.
REPEAT 1000	Do 1000 trials.
SHUFFLE B C	Mix up the hats.
SUBTRACT A C D	Subtract the shuffled hats from theset of men. A 0 will indicate that a man has received his own hat.
COUNT D =0 E	Count the number of 0's -- the number of men who received their own hats back.
SCORE E Z	Keep track of each trial result.
END	End one experiment, go back and repeat until all 1000 are complete.
HISTOGRAM Z	Produce a histogram of the trial results.

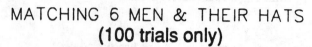

MATCHING 6 MEN & THEIR HATS
(100 trials only)

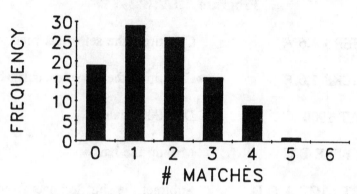

From the histogram, we see that in 81% of the trial results at least one man received his own hat back. RESAMPLING STATS will calculate this for us with the following commands:

COUNT Z >= 1 K   Determine how many trials resulted in at least one man getting his hat back.

DIVIDE K 1000 KK   Convert to a proportion.

PRINT KK   Print the results.

Example 5-6: A Compound Problem: Five or More Spades in One Bridge Hand, and Four Girls and a Boy in a Five-Child Family.

"Compound" does not necessarily mean "complicated". It means that the problem is a compound of two or more simpler problems.

A natural way to handle such a compound problem is in stages, as we saw in "Archery". If a "success" is achieved in the first stage, go on to the second stage; if not, don't go on. More specifically in this example:

Step 1. Use a bridge hand, and five coins with "heads" = "girl."

Step 2. Deal a 13-card bridge hand. Count the spades. If 5 or more spades, record "yes," otherwise "no."

Step 3. If "no" recorded in step 2, record "no," and end the experimental trial. If "yes" in step 2, throw five coins, and count "heads." If four heads, record "yes," otherwise "no."

Step 4. Repeat steps 2 and 3 a thousand times.

Step 5. Compute proportion of "yes" in step 3. This estimates the probability sought.

The RESAMPLING STATS solution to "Compound" is neither long nor difficult. We tackle it almost as if the two parts of the problem were to be solved separately. First, in a random bridge hand, we determine whether 5 spades or more are dealt, as was done in the problem "Spades." Then, IF 5 or more spades are found, proceed to GENERATE a random family of 5 children. This means that we need not GENERATE families if 5 or more spades were not dealt to the bridge hand, because a "success" is only recorded if both conditions are met. After we SCORE the number of girls in each sample of 5 children, we need only END the loop and COUNT the number of samples that had 4 girls. Since we only drew samples of children for those trials in which a bridge hand of 5 spades had already been dealt, we will have in K the number of trials out of 1000 in which both conditions were met.

Program "COMPOUND"

NUMBERS 1,52 A	Constitute a deck of 52 cards. We will let spades, the only suit we are interested in, be represented by the numbers 1,13.
REPEAT 1000	Do the following experiment 1000 times.
SHUFFLE A B	Shuffle the deck.
TAKE B 1,13 C	Deal out one hand of 13.
COUNT C between 1 13 D	Find out how many of the 13 cards are spades (spades are represented by the numbers 1-13).
IF D >= 5	If we have 5 or more spades...
GENERATE 5 1,2 E	"Generate" a family of 5, randomly selecting among girls (1's) and boys (2's).
COUNT E =1 J	Count the number of girls.
SCORE J Z	Keep track of the number of girls in each trial. Recall that we are only counting girls if we have already gotten five spades in the bridge hand.
END	End the IF condition.
END	End the experiment, go back and repeat until all 1000 trials are complete.

COUNT Z =4 K	Count the number of times we got 4 girls (and 5 or more spades).
DIVIDE K 1000 KK	Convert to a proportion.
PRINT KK	Print the results.

This completes the discussion of problems in probability -- that is, problems where we assume that the structure is known.

CHAPTER 6

INFERENTIAL STATISTICS
PART 1

INTRODUCTION

TRANSLATING SCIENTIFIC QUESTIONS INTO PROBABILISTIC AND STATISTICAL QUESTIONS

EXAMPLE 6-1: Twenty-nine Out of Fifty People Asked Say They Will Vote For The Democrat

EXAMPLE 6-2: Using Measured Data - the Bootstrap

HOW CLOSE IS THE SAMPLE MEAN OR PROPORTION TO THAT OF THE POPULATION? (CONFIDENCE INTERVALS)

INTRODUCTION

Chapters 4 and 5 discussed problems in probability theory. That is, we have been estimating the probability of a composite event resulting from a system in which we <u>know</u> the probabilities of the simple events -- the "parameters" of the situation.

Now we turn to inferential-statistical problems. These are problems in which <u>we seek to learn and estimate</u> the probabilities of a system, that is, the probabilities of its simple events and parameters. To estimate the probabilities of the system in such problems, we employ the characteristics of the sample or samples that have been drawn from it.

For further discussion on the distinction between inferential statistics and probability theory, see chapter 3.

This chapter, together with chapter 7, discusses the application of resampling statistics to hypothesis-testing problems -- that is, problems in which we evaluate various notions about the "parameters" of the universe from which the samples are drawn, employing only the characteristics of the sample, or samples, that have been drawn from it. Subsequent chapters take up estimating the strength of a relationship between two or more variables.

This chapter begins with discussion of the relationship between, on the one hand, the proportion and other statistics of a sample, and, on the other hand, the proportion and other parameters of a two-outcome (yes-no) universe from which the sample is drawn. The main practical question is: How close is an estimate of the sample mean (proportion) likely to be to the population mean (proportion)?

The mean of the universe (or the proportion, if we are speaking of two-valued "binomial situations)" is a frequent object of our interest. This chapter offers an informal proof that the mean of the sample is an "unbiased" estimator of the population mean. That is, the errors of the sample means will cancel out after repeated samples because the mean of a large number of sample means approaches the population mean. A second "law" informally proven here is that the size of the inaccuracy of a sample proportion is largest when the population proportion is near 50 percent, and smallest when it approaches zero percent or 100 percent.

Then we begin the topic of "hypothesis testing" -- does a particular sample (or samples) come from a particular universe? A two-outcome yes-no universe is discussed first. Then we move on to "measured-data" universes, which are more complex than yes-no outcomes because the variables can take on many values and because we ask somewhat more complex questions about the relationships of the samples to the universes. This topic is continued in subsequent chapters.

In a typical hypothesis-testing problem presented in this chapter, one sample of hospital patients is treated with a new drug and a second "placebo" sample is not treated. After obtaining results from the samples, the "null" or "test" or "benchmark" hypothesis would be that the resulting means of the drug and placebo samples are drawn from the same universe. This device -- the equivalent of stating that the drug had no effect on the patients -- is a special intellectual strategy developed to handle such issues. We translate the scientific question -- Does the medicine have an effect? -- into a testable statistical question -- How likely is it that the sample means come from the same universe? This process of question-translation is the crucial step in hypothesis-testing and inferential statistics. The chapter then explains how to solve these problems using resampling methods once you have formulated the proper statistical question.

TRANSLATING SCIENTIFIC QUESTIONS INTO PROBABILISTIC AND STATISTICAL QUESTIONS

Science does not begin and end with statistics. Professional statisticians are quite humble about the importance of statistics. But taking a course or two in analytical statistics has a way of going to a student's head, making one think that nothing can be proved without statistics and that anything can be proved if sophisticated statistics are used. This is the fallacy of "statistics is everything".

The fallacy of "statistics is nothing" is also dangerous. As Dunnette points out, researchers often disregard statistics because their intuition tells them that some conclusions must be so " ... on the grounds that they are intrinsically good for humanity and that they need not, therefore, meet the usual standards demanded by scientific verification.... [Psychotherapy, for example] continues to survive in spite of a lack of evidence about its effectiveness" (Dunnette, 1966, p. 346).

A social-scientific study properly begins with a general question about the nature of the social world. The scientist then must transform this question into a form that s/he can study scientifically.

Let us suppose that, by this time, the researcher has not only translated the general question into a scientific question but has also carried out the scientific investigation as an experiment or survey. Suppose further that the data that s/he has collected are not entirely clear-cut in support of firm conclusions. At this juncture, if s/he does not want to, or cannot, collect more data, the researcher may turn to inferential statistics for help.

The first step in using probability and statistics is to translate the scientific question into a statistical question. Once you know exactly which probability-statistical question you want to ask -- that is, exactly which probability you want to determine -- the rest of the work is relatively easy. The stage at which you are most likely to make mistakes is in stating the question you want to answer in probabilistic terms. Though this step is hard, it involves no mathematics. This step requires only hard, clear thinking. You cannot beg off by saying "I have no brain for math!" To flub this step is to admit that you have no brain for clear thinking, rather than no brain for mathematics.

I repeat, the hardest job in using probability statistics, and the most important, is to translate the scientific question into a form to which statistics can give a sensible answer. You must translate scientific questions into the appropriate form for statistical operations, so that you know which operations to perform. Again, this is the part of the job that requires hard, clear thinking -- though it is non-mathematical thinking -- and it is the part that someone else usually cannot easily do for you.

The best way to explain how to translate a scientific question into a statistical question is to illustrate the process.

Illustration A

As of 1964 we asked: Are doctors' beliefs about the harmfulness of cigarette smoking (and doctors' own smoking behavior) affected by the social groups among whom they live (Simon, 1967-1968)? We decided to define the doctors' reference groups as the states in which they live, because data about doctors and smoking were available state by state (Modern Medicine, 1964). We could then translate this question into an operational and testable scientific hypothesis by asking this question: Do doctors in tobacco-economy states differ from doctors in other states in their smoking, and their beliefs about smoking?

Which numbers would help us answer this question, and how do we interpret those numbers? We now were ready to ask the <u>statistical</u> question: Do doctors in tobacco-economy states "belong to the same universe" (with respect to smoking) as do other doctors? That is, do doctors in tobacco-economy states have the same characteristics -- at least, those characteristics we are interested in, smoking in this case -- as do other doctors? Later we shall see that the way to proceed is to consider the statistical hypothesis that these doctors do indeed belong to that same universe; that hypothesis and the universe will be called "benchmark hypothesis" and "benchmark universe" respectively -- or in more conventional usage, the "null hypothesis".

If the tobacco-economy doctors do indeed belong to the benchmark universe, that is, if the benchmark hypothesis is correct, then there is a 49/50 chance that doctors in some state <u>other than</u> the state in which tobacco is most important will have the highest rate of cigarette smoking. But in fact we observe that the state in which tobacco accounts for the largest proportion of the state's income -- North Carolina -- had (as of 1964) a higher proportion of doctors who smoked than any other state. (Furthermore, a lower proportion of doctors in North Carolina than in any other state said that they <u>believed</u> that smoking is a health hazard.)

Of course, it is possible that it was just <u>chance</u> that North Carolina doctors smoked most, but the chance is only 1 in 50 if the benchmark hypothesis is correct. Obviously, <u>some</u> state had to have the highest rate, and the chance for any other state was also 1 in 50. But, because our original <u>scientific</u> hypothesis was that North Carolina doctors' smoking rate would be highest, and we then observed that it was highest even though the chance was only 1 in 50, the observation became interesting and meaningful to us. It means that the chances are strong -- 49 in 50 -- that there was a connection between the importance of tobacco in the economy of a state and the rate of cigarette smoking among doctors living there (as of 1964).

To attack this problem from another direction, it would be rare for North Carolina to have the highest smoking rate for doctors if there were no special reason for it; in fact, it would occur only once in fifty times. But, if there <u>were</u> a special reason -- and we hypothesize that the tobacco economy provides the reason -- then it would <u>not</u> seem unusual or rare for North Carolina to have the highest rate; therefore we choose to believe in the not-so-unusual phenomenon, that the tobacco economy caused doctors to smoke cigarettes.

Illustration B

Does medicine CCC cure cancer? You begin with this scientific question and give the medicine to six patients who have cancer; you do not give it to six similar patients who have cancer. Your sample is only twelve people because it is simply not feasible for you to obtain a larger one. Five of six "medicine" patients get well, two of six "no medicine" patients get well. Does the medicine cure cancer? That is, if future cancer patients take the medicine, will their rate of recovery be higher than if they did not take the medicine?

One way to translate the scientific question into a statistical question is to ask: Do the "medicine" patients belong to the same universe as the "no medicine" patients? that is, we ask whether "medicine" patients still have the <u>same</u> chances of getting well from the cancer as do the "no medicine" patients, or whether the medicine has bettered the chances of those who took it and thus removed them from the original universe, with its original chances of getting well. The original universe, to which the "no medicine" patients must still belong, is the benchmark universe. Shortly we shall see that we proceed by comparing the observed results against the benchmark <u>hypothesis</u> that the "medicine" patients still belong to the benchmark <u>universe</u> -- that is, they still have the same chance of getting well as the "no medicine" patients.

We want to know whether or not the medicine does any good. This question is the same as asking whether patients who take medicine are still in the same population universe as "no medicine" patients, or whether they now belong to a different population in which patients have higher chances of getting well. To recapitulate our translations, we move from asking: Does the medicine cure cancer?; to: Do "medicine" patients have the same chance of getting well as "no medicine" patients?; and finally to: Do "medicine" patients belong to the same universe (population) as "no medicine" patients? Remember that "population" in this sense does not refer to the population at large, but rather to a group of cancer sufferers (perhaps an infinitely large group) who have given chances of getting well, on the average. Groups with different chances of getting well are called "different populations" (universes). Shortly we shall see how to answer this statistical question.

We must keep in mind that our ultimate concern in cases like this one is to predict future results of the medicine, that is, to predict whether use of the medicine will lead to a higher recovery rate than would be observed without the medicine.

Illustration C

Is method A a better method of teaching reading than method B? That is, will method A produce a higher average reading score in the future than will method B? Twenty children taught to read with method A have an average reading score of 79, whereas children taught with method B have an average score of 84. To translate this scientific question into a statistical question we ask: Do children taught with method A come from the same universe population) as children taught with method B? Again, "universe" (population) does not mean the town or social group the children come from, and indeed the experiment will make sense only if the children do come from the same population, in that sense of "population". What we want to know is whether or not the children belong to the same statistical population (universe), defined according to their reading ability, after they have studied with method A or method B.

Translating from a scientific question into a statistical question is mostly a matter of asking the probability that one or more samples come from some given benchmark universe (population). Notice that we must (at least for general scientific testing purposes) ask about a given universe whose composition we assume to be known, rather than about a range of universes, or about a universe whose properties are unknown. In fact, there is really only one question that probability statistics can answer: Given some particular benchmark universe of some stated composition, what is the probability that an observed sample comes from it? A variation of this question is: Given two (or more) samples, what is the probability that they come from the same

120

universe? In this latter case, the relevant benchmark universe is implicitly the universe whose composition is the two samples combined.

The necessity for stating the characteristics of the universe in question becomes obvious when you think about it for a moment. Probability-statistical testing adds up to comparing a sample with a particular benchmark universe, and asking whether there probably is a difference between the sample and the universe. To carry out this comparison, we ask how likely it is that the benchmark universe would produce a sample like the observed sample. But, in order to find out whether or not a universe could produce a given sample, we must ask whether or not some particular universe -- with stated characteristics -- could produce the sample. There is no doubt that some universe could produce the sample by a random process; in fact, some universe did. The only sensible question, then, is whether or not a particular universe, with stated (or known) characteristics, is likely to produce such a sample. In the case of the medicine, the universe with which we compare the sample who took the medicine is the benchmark universe to which that sample would belong if the medicine had had no effect. This comparison leads to the benchmark (null) hypothesis that the sample comes from a population in which the medicine (or other experimental treatment) seems to have no effect. It is to avoid confusion inherent in the term "null hypothesis" that I replace it with the term "benchmark hypothesis."

The concept of the benchmark (null) hypothesis is not easy to grasp. [1] The best way to learn its meaning is to see how it is used in practice. For example, we say we are willing to believe that the medicine has an effect if it seems very unlikely from the number who get well that the patients given the medicine still belong to the same benchmark universe as the patients given no medicine at all -- that is, if the benchmark hypothesis is unlikely.

Illustration D

If one plot of ground is treated with fertilizer, and another similar plot is not treated, the benchmark (null) hypothesis is that the corn raised on the treated plot is no different than the corn raised on the untreated lot -- that is, that the corn from the treated plot comes from ("belongs to") the same universe as the corn from the untreated plot. If our statistical test makes it seem very unlikely that a universe like that from which the untreated-plot corn comes would <u>also</u> produce corn such as came from the treated plot, then we are willing to believe that the fertilizer has an effect. For a psychological example, substitute the words "group of children" for "plot," "special training" for "fertilizer," and "I.Q. score" for "corn."

There is nothing sacred about the benchmark (null) hypothesis of "no difference." You could just as well test the benchmark hypothesis that the corn comes from a universe that averages 110 bushels per acre, if you have reason to be especially interested in knowing whether or not the fertilizer produces more than 110 bushels per acre. But in many cases it is reasonable to test the probability that a sample comes from the population that does not receive the special treatment of medicine, fertilizer, or training.

So far we have discussed the scientific question and the statistical question. Remember that there is always a generalization question, too: Do the statistical results from this particular sample of, say, rats apply to a universe of humans? This question can be answered only with wisdom, common sense, and general knowledge, and not with probability statistics.

> Example 6-1: Twenty-nine Out of Fifty People Asked Say They Will Vote For The Democrat. Who Will Win The Election? The Relationship Between The Sample Proportion And The Population Proportion in a Two-Outcome Universe.

You take a random sample of 50 people in Maryland and ask which party's candidate for governor they will vote for. Twenty-nine say they will vote for the Democrat. Let's say it is reasonable to assume in this case that people will do exactly what they say they will do. The statistical question then facing you is: What proportion of the voters in Maryland will vote for the Democrat in the general election?

The general answer to the statistical question is that your best guess of the proportion of the "universe" -- which is composed of voters in the general election, in this case -- will be the same as the proportion of the sample. That is, 58% = 29/50 is your best guess about the proportion that will vote Democratic. Of course, your estimate may be too high or too low in this particular case, but in the long run -- that is, if you take many samples like this one -- on the average the sample mean will equal the universe (population) proportion. In technical terms, the sample mean is an "unbiased estimate" of the population mean. "Unbiased" in this case does not mean "friendly" or "unprejudiced," but rather that on the average -- that is, in the long run, after taking repeated samples -- estimates that are too high will about balance (in percentage terms) those that are too low.

The statement that the sample mean is an unbiased estimate of the population mean holds for all kinds of samples, proportions of two-outcome (Democrat-Republican) events (as in this case) and also the means of measured-data universes (heights, speeds, and so on) that we will come to later.

But, you object, I have only said that this is so; I haven't proven it. Quite right. Now we will go beyond this simple assertion, though we won't reach the level of formal proof. The pages from here to the end of the chapter encompass the second hardest section of the book. Nevertheless, I don't think you'll find it unpleasantly difficult. Furthermore, all of this discussion applies to conventional analytic statistical theory as well as the resampling approach, though the topic is usually glossed over in discussion of the conventional approach. [2]

We want to know why the average of repeated sample means (proportions) tends to equal the universe proportion. Consider a population of one thousand voters. You split the population into random sub-populations of 500 voters each; let's call these sub-populations by the name "samples". Almost inevitably, the proportions voting Democratic in the samples will not exactly equal the "true" proportions in the population. (Why not? Well, why should they? There is no reason why they should.) But if the sample proportions do not equal the population proportion, we can say that the extent of the difference between the two sample proportions and the population proportion will be <u>identical but in the opposite direction</u>.

If the population proportion is 600/1000 = 60%, and one sample's proportion is 340/500 = 68%, then the other sample's proportion must be (600-340 = 260)/500 = 52%. So if in the very long run you would choose each of these two samples about half the time (as you would if you selected between the two samples randomly) the average of the sample proportions would be (68% + 52%)/2 = 60%. This shows that on the average the sample proportion is a fair and unbiased estimate of the population proportion -- if the sample is half the size of the population.

If we now sub-divide each of our two samples of 500 (each of which was half the population size) into equal-size subsamples of 250 each, the same argument will hold for the proportions of the samples of 250 with respect to the sample of 500: The proportion of a 250-voter sample is an unbiased estimate of the proportion of the 500-voter sample from which it is drawn. It seems inductively reasonable, then, that if the proportion of a 250-voter sample is an unbiased estimate of the 500-voter sample from which it is drawn, and the proportion of a 500-voter sample is an unbiased estimate of the 1000-voter population, then the proportion of a 250-voter sample should be an unbiased estimate of the population proportion. And if so, this argument should hold for samples of 1/2 x 250 = 125, and so on -- in fact for <u>any</u> size sample.

The argument given above is not a rigorous formal proof. But I doubt that the non-mathematician needs, or will benefit from, a more formal proof of this proposition. You are more likely to be persuaded if you demonstrate this proposition to yourself experimentally in the following manner:

Step 1. Let "1-6" = Democrat, "7-10" = Republican

Step 2. Choose a sample of, say, ten random numbers, and record the proportion Democrat (the sample proportion).

Step 3. Repeat step 2 a thousand times.

Step 4. Compute the mean of the sample proportions, and compare it to the population proportion of 60%. This result should be close enough to reassure you that <u>on the average</u> the sample proportion is an "unbiased" estimate of the population proportion, though in any particular sample it may be substantially off in either direction.

CONFIDENCE INTERVALS: HOW CLOSE IS THE SAMPLE PROPORTION OR MEAN TO THE POPULATION PROPORTION OR MEAN?

Example 6-1 cont.: The Two-Outcome (Binomial) Case

It is all very well to say that <u>on the average</u> the sample proportion equals the population proportion. But what about the proportion of any <u>particular</u> sample? How inaccurate is it likely to be?

If we knew the <u>population</u> proportion, we could easily determine how inaccurate the <u>sample</u> proportion is likely to be. If, for example, we wanted to know about the likely inaccuracy of the proportion of a sample of 100 voters drawn from a population of a million that is 60% Democratic, we could simply simulate drawing (say) 200 samples of 100 voters from such a universe, and examine the average inaccuracy of the 200 sample proportions.

But in fact we do <u>not</u> know the characteristics of the actual universe. Rather, the nature of the actual universe is what we seek to learn about. Of course, if the amount of variation among samples were <u>the same no matter what</u> the Republican-Democrat proportions in the universe, the issue would still be simple, because we could then estimate the average inaccuracy of the sample proportion for any universe and then assume that it would hold for our universe. But it is reasonable to suppose that the amount of variation among samples will be different for different Democrat-Republican proportions in the universe.

Let us first see why the amount of variation among samples drawn from a given universe is different with different relative proportions of the events in the universe. Consider a universe of 999,999 Democrats and one Republican. Most samples of 100 taken from this universe will contain 100 Democrats. A few (and only a very, very few) samples will contain 99 Democrats and one Republican. So the biggest possible difference between the sample proportion and the population proportion (99.9999%) is less than one percent (for the very few samples of 99% democrats). And most of the time the difference will only be the tiny difference between a sample of 100 Democrats (sample proportion = 100%), and the population proportion of 99.9999%.

Compare the above to the possible difference between a sample of 100 from a universe of half a million Republicans and half a million Democrats. At worst a sample could be off by as much as 50% (if it got zero Republicans or zero Democrats), and at best it is unlikely to get exactly 50 of each. So it will almost always be off by 1% or more.

It seems, therefore, intuitively reasonable (and in fact it is true) that the likely difference between a sample proportion and the population proportion is greatest with a 50%-50% universe, least with a 0%-100% universe, and somewhere in between for probabilities, in the fashion of Figure 6-1.

Figure 6-1
Relationship Between the Population Proportion
and the Likely Error in a Sample

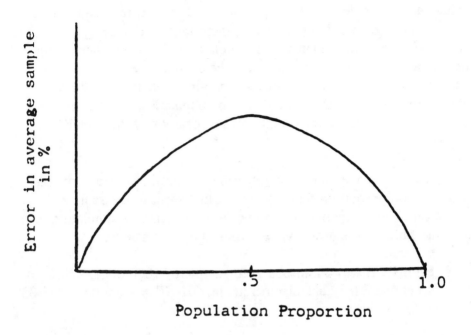

Figure 6-1 and the reasoning behind it help us some -- but only some. If we have a sample of 100 observations, we can know what the average error is if the population proportion is 0 or .5 or anything else in between. But we don't know which it is. So what should we do?

No single logically-correct answer exists, I'm sorry to say. Or, at least there is no logically-correct answer for any particular sample. But there is a logically-correct way to proceed if you think of this sample as just one of the many samples you will draw in your lifetime, and if you wish to be as correct as you can on the average over your lifetime. Furthermore, this long-run answer is not likely to be very much in error for any one particular sample.

Sound procedure for estimating the variability of the proportion of two-outcome samples is as follows: Assume that the extent of variation in the sample is your best estimate of the amount of variation in the population. More specifically, let us assume that the probability of two randomly-drawn elements being the same rather than different is similar in the sample and the population. Of course, this assumption might be incorrect in either direction; there might be more or less variation in the sample than in the population. But over many samples this will average out. Furthermore, if the sample size is, say, ten or more observations in a two-outcome sampling situation, the difference in variability between the sample and the population is not likely to have much effect on your estimate of the accuracy of the population proportion.

Let us, then, estimate by experimentation the accuracy of the population proportion on the assumption that we take the sample proportion to be the population proportion's estimate -- simulating how much the sample proportion varies from sample to sample.

Step 1. Based on an observed sample of 100 voters, 57 of whom said they are Democrats, let "01-57" = Democrat, "58-00" = Republican.

Step 2. Draw a sample of the 100 two-digit numbers. Calculate and record the proportion.

Step 3. Repeat step 2 one hundred times.

Steps 1-3 are done quickly with RESAMPLING STATS.

Step 4. Rank the observed sample proportions from highest to lowest, as in column 3 of Table 6-1, and number them by rank as in Column 2. Calculate the difference between the proportion in each experiment and the observed proportion of 57%, as in Column 4.

Step 5. Inspect column 2 in Table 6-1 to learn the probability that the sample proportion will diverge from the population proportion by any given amount of divergence you are interested

128

in. For example, in 25 percent of the experiments (rank 76 and below; see Column 2) the sample proportion will be 4% or more below the population proportion if the population proportion is 57%, and in 50% of the cases the sample proportion will be at least 4% below or 3% above the population proportion. Only 5% of the time the sample proportion will be 7% below a population proportion of 57%, and 10% of the time the sample proportion will be 7% below or 8% above the population proportion. Steps 4 and 5 also can easily be done with RESAMPLING STATS.

Any two arbitrary (usually symmetrical) points around the estimated population mean or proportion are called "confidence limits". For example, 65% and 50% are called the 90% confidence limits around the population proportion of 57% for a sample size of 100. (This is another way of viewing the numbers given just above; 65% = 57% + 8%, and 50% = 57% - 7%). That is, 90% of the time one could expect that the population proportion will be within those limits, given a sample such as we have observed. That is, you can say "with confidence" that there is a 90% chance that 65% and 50% "bracket" the proportion of the "true" population from which the sample of 100 was drawn. Or to put it another way, your "confidence level" is 90% that the population proportion is somewhere between those two proportions of 65% and 50%.

Table 6-1
Differences Between Observed Sample Proportion and Proportion in 100 Randomly Drawn Samples
(Observed Proportion = 57%)

Trial Number	Rank Number	Sample Prop.	Difference Between Col. (3) and 57%
(1)	(2)	(3)	(4)
78	1	74	17%
39	2	67	10%
32	3	66	9%
57	4	65	8%
90	5	65	8%
25	6	64	7%
91	7	64	7%
8	8	63	6%
51	9	63	6%
76	10	63	6%
84	11	63	6%
86	12	63	6%
7	13	62	5%
14	14	62	5%
19	15	62	5%
65	16	62	5%
13	17	61	4%
30	18	61	4%
36	19	61	4%
61	20	61	4%
66	21	61	4%
77	22	61	4%
94	23	61	4%
15	24	60	3%
16	25	60	3%
52	26	60	3%
59	27	60	3%
71	28	60	3%
99	29	60	3%
20	30	59	2%
23	31	59	2%
24	32	59	2%
28	33	59	2%
33	34	59	2%

Table 6-1 (Continued)

Trial Number	Rank Number	Sample Prop.	Difference Between Col. (3) and 57%
38	35	59	2%
74	36	59	2%
87	37	59	2%
1	38	58	1%
6	39	58	1%
17	40	58	1%
26	41	58	1%
47	42	58	1%
68	43	58	1%
75	44	58	1%
95	45	58	1%
3	46	57	0%
4	47	57	0%
18	48	57	0%
49	49	57	0%
80	50	57	0%
22	51	56	-1%
42	52	56	-1%
50	53	56	-1%
64	54	56	-1%
68	55	56	-1%
73	56	56	-1%
85	57	56	-1%
5	58	55	-2%
43	59	55	-2%
55	60	55	-2%
60	61	55	-2%
69	62	55	-2%
70	63	55	-2%
79	64	55	-2%
83	65	55	-2%
89	66	55	-2%
93	67	55	-2%
100	68	55	-2%
12	69	54	-3%
31	70	54	-3%
35	71	54	-3%
72	72	54	-3%
82	73	54	-3%
88	74	54	-3%

Table 6-1 (Continued)

Trial Number	Rank Number	Sample Prop.	Difference Between Col. (3) and 57%
2	75	53	-4%
27	76	53	-4%
40	77	53	-4%
44	78	53	-4%
45	79	53	-4%
53	80	53	-4%
92	81	53	-4%
10	82	52	-5%
11	83	52	-5%
21	84	52	-5%
29	85	52	-5%
37	86	52	-5%
41	87	52	-5%
46	88	52	-5%
64	89	52	-5%
67	90	52	-5%
81	91	52	-5%
48	92	51	-6%
56	93	51	-6%
62	94	51	-6%
73	95	50	-7%
96	96	50	-7%
98	97	50	-7%
34	98	49	-8%
97	99	49	-8%
9	100	48	-9%

Example 6-2: Using Measured Data - the Bootstrap. A Feed Merchant Experiences Varied Pig Weight Gains With a New Ration and Wants to be Safe in Advertising an Average Weight Gain

A feed merchant decides to experiment with a new pig ration - ration A - on twelve pigs. To obtain a random sample, he provides twelve customers (selected at random) with sufficient food for one pig. After 4 weeks, the 12 pigs experience an average gain of 508 ounces. The weight gains of the individual pigs are as follows: 496, 544, 464, 416, 512, 560, 608, 544, 480, 466, 512, 496.

The merchant sees that the ration produces results that are quite variable (from a low of 466 ounces to a high of 560 ounces) and is therefore reluctant to advertise an average weight gain of 508 ounces. He speculates that a different sample of pigs might well produce a different average weight gain.

Unfortunately, it is impractical to sample additional pigs to gain additional information about the universe of weight gains. The merchant must rely on the data already gathered. How can these data be used to tell us more about the sampling variability of the average weight gain?

Recalling that all we know about the universe of weight gains is the sample we have observed, we can replicate that sample millions of times, creating a "pseudo-universe" that embodies all our knowledge about the real universe. We can then draw additional samples from this pseudo-universe and see how they behave.

More specifically, we replicate each observed weight gain millions of times -- we can imagine writing each result that many times on separate pieces of paper -- then shuffle those weight gains and pick out a sample of 12. Average the weight gain for that sample, and record the result. Take repeated samples, and record the result for each. We can then make a histogram of the results; it might look something like this:

Figure 6-2

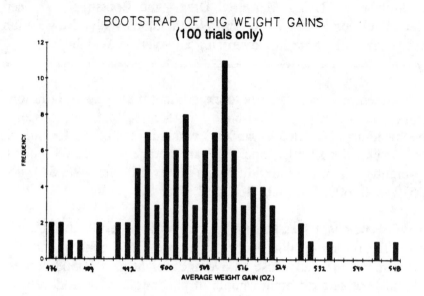

BOOTSTRAP OF PIG WEIGHT GAINS
(100 trials only)

Though we do not know the true average weight gain, we can use this histogram to estimate the bounds within which it falls. The merchant can consider various weight gains for advertising purposes, and estimate the probability that the true weight gain falls below that value. For example, he might wish to advertise a weight gain of 500 ounces. Examining the histogram, we see that 27% of our samples yielded weight gains less than 500 ounces. The merchant might wish to choose a lower weight gain to advertise, to reduce the risk of overstating the effectiveness of the ration.

This example illustrates the "bootstrap" method, one of the two techniques (the other is the "sampled permutation test" or "randomization test") that especially fit with the resampling approach. By re-using our original sample many times (and using nothing else), we are able to make inferences about the population from which the sample came. This problem would conventionally be addressed with the "t-test".

USING RESAMPLING STATS

Solving this problem with RESAMPLING STATS closely follows the above steps:

Program "PIGFOOD"

NUMBERS (496 544 464 416 512 560 608 544 480 466 512 496) A	Record the data for pig weight gains in "A".
REPEAT 1000	Do 1000 trials or "resamples".
SAMPLE 12 A B	Take a sample of 12 with replacement from "A" and put it in "B".
MEAN B C	Find the resample average.
SCORE C Z	Keep track of the results of each resample.
END	End the loop for one resample, go back and repeat until all 1000 resamples have been completed and scored.
HISTOGRAM Z	Generate a histogram of the results. (see fig. 6-2)

NOTES:

[1]   The classic discussion of the null hypothesis is by R.A. Fisher in his <u>The Design of Experiments</u> (1935, 1951), but even that discussion is not at all satisfactory. Another useful treatment is by J. Neyman (1950, Chapter 5), who substitutes the term "test hypothesis" for "null hypothesis", however. Still, this concept is among the slipperiest in all scientific research, and perhaps the hardest to learn. Don't despair if the notion eludes you at first. It will come clear as you work with it.

[2]   An excellent exception is Mosteller, Rourke and Thomas, 1970, pp 431- 441.

CHAPTER 7

THE STATISTICS OF HYPOTHESIS-TESTING
WITH COUNTED DATA

INTRODUCTION

EXAMPLE 7-1 Does Irradiation Affect the Sex Ratio in Fruit Flies?

EXAMPLE 7-2 Do Any of Four Treatments Affect the Sex Ratio in Fruit Flies?

EXAMPLE 7-3 A Public-Opinion Poll (Is the Proportion of a Population Greater than a Given Value?)

EXAMPLE 7-4 Comparison of Possible Cancer Cure to Placebo Effect

EXAMPLE 7-5 Do Four Psychological Treatments Differ in Effectiveness? (Do Several Binomial Samples Differ in Their Proportions?)

EXAMPLE 7-6 Is One Pig Ration More Effective Than the Other? (Testing For a Difference in Means With a Two-by-Two Classification.)

EXAMPLE 7-7 Comparison of Pairs of Pigs

INTRODUCTION

Having reviewed how to convert hypothesis-testing problems into statistically testable questions in Chapter 6, we now must ask: How does one employ resampling methods to make the statistical test? As is always the case when using resampling statistics, there is no unique series of steps by which to proceed. The single criterion in assessing the model is whether it accurately simulates the actual event. With hypothesis-testing problems, any number of models may be correct, but generally speaking, the model that makes fullest use of the quantitative information available from the data is the best model.

When attempting to deduce the characteristics of a universe from sample data, or when asking whether a sample was drawn from a particular universe, a crucial issue is whether a "one-tailed test" or a "two-tailed test" should be applied. That is, in examining the results of our resampling experiment based on the benchmark universe, do we examine both ends of the frequency distribution, or just one? If there is strong reason to believe a priori that the difference between the benchmark (null) universe and the sample will be in a given direction, -- for example if you hypothesize that the sample mean will be smaller than the mean of the benchmark universe -- then you should employ a one-tailed test. If you do not have strong basis for such a prediction, then use the two-tailed test. As an example, when a scientist tests a new medication, his hypothesis would be that the number of patients who get well will be higher in the treated group than in the control group. Thus, he applies the one-tailed test.

This chapter also introduces the concept of "significance levels". This term refers to the probability that the assumed benchmark universe would give rise to a sample as extreme as the observed sample - in other words, the probability that an observed sample is different from the universe, or the probability that the sample has different properties than the universe. Of course, whether a one-tailed or two-tailed test is used will influence your significance level, and this is why great care must be taken in making that choice.

Now let us begin the actual statistical testing of various sorts of hypotheses about samples and populations.

Example 7-1: Does Irradiation Affect the Sex Ratio in Fruit Flies? (Where the Benchmark Universe Mean (Proportion) is Known, is the Mean (Proportion) of the Population Affected by the Treatment?) (Program "Fruitfly")

You think you have developed a technique for irradiating the genes of fruit flies so that the sex ratio of the offspring will not be half males and half females. In the first twenty cases you treat, there are fourteen males and six females. Does this experimental result confirm that the irradiation does work?

First convert the scientific question -- whether or not the treatment affects the sex distribution -- into a probability-statistical question: Is the observed sample likely to have come from a universe in which the sex ratio is one male to one female? The benchmark (null) hypothesis, then, is that the treatment makes no difference and the sample comes from the one-to-one universe. (The concept of the benchmark hypothesis was discussed in Chapter 4.) Therefore, we investigate how likely a one-to-one universe is to produce a distribution of fourteen or more of just one sex.

A coin has a one-to-one (one out of two) chance of coming up tails. Therefore, we might flip a coin in groups of twenty flips, and count the number of heads in each twenty flips. Or we can use a random number table. The following steps will produce a sound estimate:

Step 1. Let "heads" = males, "tails" = females.

Step 2. Flip twenty coins and count the number of males. If 14 or more males occur, record "yes." Also, if 6 or fewer males occur, record "yes" because this means we have gotten 14 or more females. Otherwise, record "no".

Step 3. Repeat step 2 perhaps 100 times.

Step 4. Calculate the proportion "yes" in the 100 trials. This proportion estimates the probability that a fruit-fly population with a propensity to produce 50% males will by chance produce as many as 14 or as few as 6 males in a sample of 20 flies.

Table 7-1 shows the results obtained in twenty-five trials of twenty flips each.

Table 7-1								
Results From 25 Random Trials for "Fruitfly" Problem								
Trial of 20 Coin Flips (1)	# of Heads (2)	>=14 or <=6 (3)	Trial of 20 Coin Flips (1)	# of Heads (2)	>=14 or <=6 (3)	Trial of 20 Coin Flips (1)	# of Heads (2)	>=14 or <=6 (3)
1	11	no	10	10	no	19	13	no
2	12	no	11	10	no	20	10	no
3	8	no	12	10	no	21	11	no
4	12	no	13	9	no	22	14	yes
5	12	no	14	9	no	23	9	no
6	7	no	15	12	no	24	7	no
7	9	no	16	7	no	25	10	no
8	8	no	17	14	yes			
9	6	yes	18	12	no			

In two of the twenty-five trials (8 percent) there were fourteen or more heads, which we shall call "males," and in one of the twenty-five trials (4 percent) there were only six heads, meaning there were fourteen tails ("females"). We can therefore estimate that, even if the treatment does <u>not</u> affect the sex and the births over a long period are really one to one, we would get fourteen or more of one sex or the other three out of twenty-five times (12 percent). Therefore, finding fourteen males out of twenty births is not overwhelming evidence that the treatment has any effect, though it is suggestive.

How accurate is the estimate? Seventy-five more trials were made, and of the 100 trials ten contained fourteen or more "males" (10 percent), and seven trials contained fourteen or more "females" (7 percent), a total of 17 percent. So the first twenty-five trials gave a fairly reliable indication. As a matter of fact, analytically-based computation (not explained here) shows that the probability of getting fourteen or more females out of twenty births is .057 and, of course, the same for fourteen or more males from a one-to-one universe, implying a total probability of .114 of getting fourteen or more males or females.

The key step in the RESAMPLING STATS program "Fruitfly" is to GENERATE 20 numbers with two equally-likely outcomes: "1" to stand for a male, and "2" to stand for a female. This simulates randomly choosing 20 fruit flies on the benchmark assumption -- the "null hypothesis" -- that each fruit fly has an equal chance of being a male or female. Now we want to discover the chances of getting over 13 (i.e., 14 or more) males or over 13 females under these conditions. So we COUNT the number of males in each random sample and then keep SCORE of this number for each sample.

After one thousand samples have been drawn, we COUNT how often there were more than 13 males and then count the number of times there were fewer than 7 males (because if there were fewer than 7 males there must have been more than 13 females). When we ADD the two results together we have the probability that the results obtained from the sample of irradiated fruit flies would be obtained from a random sample of fruit flies.

Program "FRUITFLY"

REPEAT 1000	Do 1000 experiments
GENERATE 20 1,2 A	Generate randomly 20 1's and 2's, put them in A.
COUNT A =1 B	Count the number of 1's (males), put that result in B.
SCORE B Z	Keep track of each trial result in Z.
END	End one trial, go back and repeat until all 1000 trials are complete.
HISTOGRAM Z	Produce a histogram of the trial results.

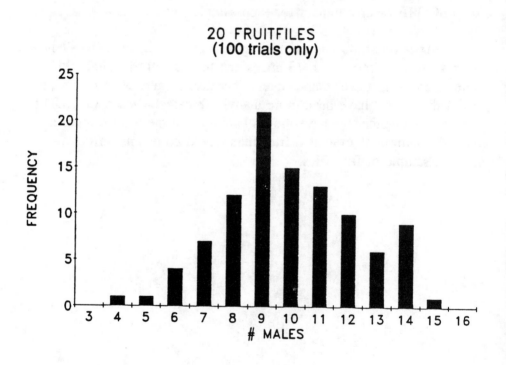

20 FRUITFILES
(100 trials only)

From this histogram, we see that in 16% of the trials, the number of males was 14 or more, or 6 or fewer. We can use RESAMPLING STATS to calculate this for us by tacking on the following commands to the above program:

COUNT Z >=14 J	Determine the number of trials in which we had 14 or more males.
COUNT Z <=6 K	Determine the number of trials in which we had 6 or fewer males.
ADD J K L	Add the two results together.
DIVIDE L 1000 LL	Convert to a proportion.
PRINT LL	Print the results.

Notice that the strength of the evidence for the effectiveness of the radiation treatment depends upon the original question: whether or not the treatment had any effect on the sex of the fruit fly. If there were reason to believe at the start that the treatment could increase only the number of males, then we would focus our attention on the result that in only two of our first twenty-five trials were fourteen or more males. There would then be only a 2/25 = .08 probability of getting the observed results by chance if the treatment really has no effect, rather than the weaker odds against obtaining fourteen or more of either males or females.

Therefore, whether you decide to figure the odds of just fourteen or more males (what is called a "one-tail test") or for fourteen or more males plus fourteen or more females (a "two-tail test"), depends upon your advance knowledge of the subject. If you have no reason to believe that the treatment will have an effect only in the direction of creating more males and if you figure the odds for the one-tail test anyway, then you will be kidding yourself. Theory comes to bear here. If you have a strong hypothesis, deduced from a strong theory, that there will be more males, then you should figure one-tail odds, but if you have no such theory you should figure the weaker two-tail odds. [1]

THE CONCEPT OF SIGNIFICANCE

"Significance level" is a common term in probability statistics. It corresponds roughly to the probability that the assumed benchmark universe could give rise to a sample as extreme as the observed sample by chance. The results of Example 7-1 would be phrased as follows: The hypothesis that the radiation treatment affects the sex of the fruit fly offspring is accepted as true at the probability level of .16 (sometimes stated as the 16 percent level of significance). (A more common way of expressing this idea would be to say that the hypothesis is <u>not rejected</u> at the .16 probability level [or the 16 percent level of significance]. But "not rejected" and "accepted" really do mean much the same thing, despite some arguments to the contrary.) This kind of statistical work is called hypothesis testing.

The question of <u>which</u> significance level should be said to be "significant" is difficult. How great must a coincidence be before you refuse to believe that it is only a coincidence? It has been conventional in social science to say that if the probability that something happens by chance is less than 5 percent, it is significant. But sometimes the stiffer standard of 1 percent is used. Actually, <u>any</u> fixed cut-off significance level is arbitrary. (And even the whole notion of saying that a hypothesis "is true" or "is not true" is sometimes not useful.)

Before leaving this example, let us review our intellectual strategy in handling the problem. First we observe a result (14 males in 20 flies) which differs from the proportion of the benchmark population (50% males). Because we have treated this sample with irradiation and observed a result that differs from the untreated benchmark-population's mean, we speculate that the irradiation caused the sample to differ from the untreated population. We wish to check on whether this speculation is correct.

When asking whether this speculation is correct, we are implicitly asking whether future irradiation would also produce a proportion of males higher than 50%. That is, we are implicitly asking whether irradiated flies would produce more samples with male

144

proportions as high as 14/20 than would occur by chance in the absence of irradiation.

If samples as far away as 14/20 from the population mean would occur frequently by chance, then we would not be impressed with that experimental evidence as proof that irradiation affects the sex ratio. Hence we set up a model that will tell us the frequency with which such samples as 14 or more males out of 20 births would be observed by chance. Carrying out the resampling procedure tells us that perhaps a tenth of the time such samples would be observed by chance. That is not frequent, but it is not infrequent either. Hence we would probably conclude that the evidence is provocative enough to justify further experimentation, but not so strong that we should immediately believe in the truth of this speculation.

Example 7-2: Do Any of Four Treatments Affect the Sex Ratio in Fruit Flies? (When the Benchmark Universe Proportion is Known, Is the Proportion of the Binomial Population Affected by Any of the Treatments?) (Program "4treat")

Suppose that, instead of trying just one type of radiation treatment on the flies, as in Example 7-1, you try four different treatments, which we shall label A, B, C, and D. In treatment A you get fourteen males and six females, but in treatments B, C, and D you get ten, eleven, and ten males, respectively. It is immediately obvious that there is no reason to think that treatment B, C, or D affects the sex ratio. But what about treatment A?

A frequent and dangerous mistake made by young scientists is to scrounge around in the data for the most extreme observation and then to treat it as if it were the only observation made. In the context of this example, it would be fallacious to think that the probability of the fourteen-males-to-six females split observed for treatment A is the same as the probability that we figured for a single experiment in Example 7-1. Instead, we must consider that our benchmark universe is composed of four sets of twenty trials, each trial having a 50-50 probability of being male. We can consider that our previous trials 1-4 in Example 7-

1 constitute a <u>single</u> new trial, and each subsequent set of four previous trials constitute another new trial. We then ask how likely a new trial of our sets of twenty flips is to produce <u>one</u> set with fourteen or more of one or the other sex.

Let us make the procedure explicit, but using random numbers instead of coins this time:

Step 1. Let "1-5" = males, "6-0" = females

Step 2. Choose four groups of twenty numbers. If for <u>any</u> group there are 14 or more males, record "yes"; if 13 or less, record "no".

Step 3. Repeat perhaps 1000 times.

Step 4. Calculate the proportion "yes" in the 1000 trials. This proportion estimates the probability that a fruit fly population with a proportion of 50% males will produce as many as 14 males in at least one of four samples of 20 flies.

We begin the trials with data as follows:

Table 7-2 Number of "Males" in Groups of 20 (Based on Random Numbers)					
Trial Number	Group A	Group B	Group C	Group D	Yes/No >= 14 or <= 6
1	11	12	8	12	No
2	12	7	9	8	No
3	6	10	10	10	Yes
4	9	9	12	7	No
5	14	12	13	10	Yes
6	11	14	9	7	Yes

In two of the six trials, more than one sample shows 14 or more males. Another trial shows fourteen or more _females_. Without even concerning ourselves about whether we should be looking at males or females, or just males, or needing to do more trials, we can see that it would be _very common indeed_ to have one of four treatments show fourteen or more of one sex just by chance. This discovery clearly indicates that a result that would be fairly unusual (three in twenty-five) for one sample alone is commonplace in one of four observed samples.

A key point of the RESAMPLING STATS program "4TREAT" is that each sample consists of _four sets_ of 20 randomly generated hypothetical fruit flies. And if we consider 1000 samples, we will be examining 4000 sets of 20 fruit flies.

In each trial we GENERATE up to 4 random samples of 20 fruit flies, and for each, we count the number of males ("1"s) and then check whether that group has more than 13 of either sex (actually, more than 13 "1"s or less than 7 "1"s). If it does, then we SET J to 1, which informs us that for this sample, at least 1 group of 20 fruit flies had results as unusual as the results from the fruit flies exposed to the four treatments.

After the 1000 runs are made, we count the number of trials where one sample had a group of fruit flies with 14 or more of either sex, and PRINT the results.

Program "4TREAT"

REPEAT 1000	Do 1000 experiments.
COPY (0) J	J indicates whether we have obtained a trial group with 14 or more of either sex. We start at 0 (= no).
REPEAT 4	Repeat the following steps 4 times to constitute 4 trial groups of 20 flies each.
GENERATE 20 1,2 A	Generate randomly 20 1's and 2's and put them in A; let 1 = male.
COUNT A =1 B	Count the number of males, put the result in B.
IF B >= 14	If the result is 14 or more males, then COPY (1) J
COPY (1) J	Set the indicator to 1.
END	End the IF condition.
IF B <= 6	If the result is 6 or fewer males (the same as 14 or more females), then
COPY (1) J	Set the indicator to 1.
END	End the IF condition.

END	End the procedure for one group, go back and repeat until all four groups have been done.
SCORE J Z	J now tells us whether we got a result as extreme as that observed (J = 1 if we did, J = 0 if not). We must keep track in Z of this result for each experiment.
END	End one experiment, go back and repeat until all 1000 are complete.
COUNT Z =1 K	Count the number of experiments in which we had results as extreme as those observed.
DIVIDE K 1000 KK	Convert to a proportion.
PRINT KK	Print the result.

In one set of 1000 trials, there were more than 13 or less than 7 males 33% of the time -- clearly not an unusual occurrence.

Example 7-3: A Public-Opinion Poll (Is the Proportion of a Population Greater Than a Given Value?) (Program "CABLEPOL")

A municipal official wants to determine whether a <u>majority</u> of the town's residents are for or against the awarding of a cable-television franchise, and he asked you to take a poll. You judged that the telephone book was a fair representation of the universe in which the politician was interested, and you decided to interview by telephone. Of a sample of fifty people who expressed opinions, thirty said "yes" they were for the plan and twenty said "no", they were against it. How conclusively do the results show that the people in town want cable television?

Now comes some necessary subtle thinking in the interpretation of what seems like a simple problem. Notice that our aim in the analysis is to avoid the mistake of saying the town favors the plan when in fact it does not favor the plan. Our chance of making this mistake is greatest when the voters are evenly split, so we choose as the benchmark (null) hypothesis that 50 percent of the town does not want the plan. This statement really means that "50 percent or more do not want the plan." We could assess the probability of obtaining our result from a population that is split (say) 52-48 against, but such a probability would necessarily be even smaller, and we are primarily interested in assessing the maximum probability of being wrong. If the maximum probability of error turns out to be inconsequential, then we need not worry about less likely errors.

This problem is very much like the one-group fruit fly-irradiation problem in Example 7-1. The only difference is that now we are comparing the observed sample against an arbitrary value of 50% (because that is the break-point in a situation where the majority decides) whereas in the fruit fly example we compared the observed sample against the normal population proportion (also 50%, because that is the normal proportion of males). But it really does not matter <u>why</u> we are comparing the observed sample to the figure of 50%; the procedure is the same in both cases. (Please notice that there is nothing special about the 50% figure; the same procedure would be followed for 20% or 85%.)

In brief, we a) designate "1-5" as "no" in the random-number table, "6-0" as "yes", b) count the number of "yes'es" and "no's" in the first fifty numbers, c) repeat for perhaps a hundred trials, then d) count the proportion of the trials in which a 50-50 universe would produce thirty or more "yes" answers.

In operational steps, the procedure is as follows:

Step 1. "1-5" = no, "6-0" = yes.

Step 2. In 50 random numbers, count the "yeses", and record "false positive" if 30 or more "yeses".

Step 3. Repeat step 2 perhaps 100 times.

Step 4. Calculate the proportion of experimental trials showing "false positive". This estimates the probability that as many as 30 "yeses" would be observed by chance in a sample of 50 people if half (or more) are really against the plan.

In Table 7-3, we see the results of twenty trials; 4 of 20 times (20%) 30 or more "yeses" were observed by chance. So our "significance level" is 20%, which is normally too high to feel confident that our poll results are reliable. This is the probability that as many as thirty of fifty people would say "yes" by chance if the population were "really" split evenly. (If the population were split so that more than 50 percent were against the plan, the probability would be even less that the observed results would occur by chance. In this sense, the benchmark hypothesis is conservative).

Table 7-3
Results of Twenty Random Trials for Problem "Cablepol"

Trial	Number of "Noes"	Number of "Yeses"	Trials With >=30 "Yeses"
1	23	27	
2	25	25	
3	26	24	
4	22	28	
5	22	28	
6	20	30	+
7	25	25	
8	21	29	
9	28	22	
10	19	31	+
11	28	22	
12	19	31	+
13	18	32	+
14	23	27	
15	34	16	
16	27	23	
17	22	28	
18	26	24	
19	28	22	
20	27	23	

On the other hand, if we had been counting "1-5" as "yes" instead of "no", there would only have been one "false positive". This indicates how samples can vary just by chance.

Taken together, the evidence suggests that the mayor would be wise not to place very much confidence in the poll results, but rather ought to act with caution or else take a bigger sample of voters.

The RESAMPLING STATS program "Cablepol" GENERATEs samples of 50 "voters" on the assumption that only 50 percent are in favor of the franchise. Then it COUNTs the number of samples where over 29 (30 or more) of the 50 respondents said they were in favor of the franchise. (That is, we use a "one-tailed test".) The result in KK is the chance of a "false positive", that is, 30 or more people saying they favor a franchise when support for the proposal is actually split evenly down the middle.

Program "CABLEPOL"

REPEAT 1000	Do 1000 trials.
GENERATE 50 1,2 A	Generate randomly 50 1's and 2's, put them in A. Let 1 = yes and 2 = no.
COUNT A =1 B	Count the number of yeses, put the result in B.
SCORE B Z	Keep track of each trial result in Z.
END	End the trial, go back and repeat until all 1000 trials are complete, then proceed.
HISTOGRAM Z	Produce a histogram of the trial results.

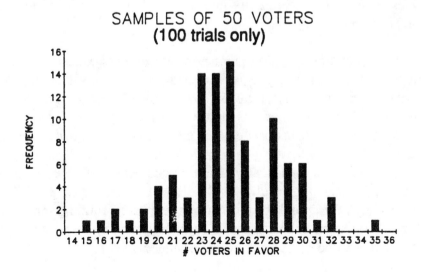

SAMPLES OF 50 VOTERS
(100 trials only)

153

From this histogram, we see that 11% of our trials had 30 or more voters in favor, despite the fact that they were drawn from a population that was split 50-50. RESAMPLING STATS will calculate this proportion directly if we add the following commands to the above:

COUNT Z >= 30 K   Determine how many trials had 30 or more in favor.

DIVIDE K 1000 KK   Convert to a proportion.

PRINT KK   Print the result.

Example 7-4: Comparison of Possible Cancer Cure to Placebo Effect (Do Two Binomial Populations Differ in Their Proportions (Program "CANCER").

Example 7-1 used an observed sample of male and female fruit flies to test the benchmark (null) hypothesis that the flies came from a universe with a one-to-one sex ratio. Now we want to compare two samples with each other, rather than comparing one sample with a hypothesized universe. That is, in this example we are not comparing one sample to a benchmark universe, but rather asking whether both samples come from the same universe. The universe from which both samples come, if both belong to the same universe, may be thought of as the benchmark universe, in this case.

The scientific question is whether pill P cures cancer. A researcher gave the pill to six patients selected randomly from a group of twelve cancer patients; of the six, five got well. He gave an inactive placebo to the other six patients, and two of them got well. Does the evidence justify a conclusion that the pill has a curative effect?

(An identical statistical example would serve for an experiment on methods of teaching reading to children. In such a case the researcher would respond to inconclusive results by running the experiment on more subjects, but in cases like the cancer-pill example the researcher often cannot obtain more subjects.)

We can answer the question as stated by <u>combining</u> the two samples and testing both samples against the resulting combined universe. In this case, the universe is twelve subjects, seven (5 + 2) of whom got well. Given such a universe, then, how likely would it be to produce two samples as far apart as five of six, and two of six, patients who get well? In other words, how often will two samples of six subjects each drawn from a universe in which 7/12 of the patients get well, be as far apart as 5 - 2 = 3 patients in favor of the sample designated "pill"? This is obviously a one-tail test, for there is no reason to believe that the pill group might do <u>less</u> well than the placebo group.

We might construct a twelve-sided die, seven of whose sides are marked "get well". Or we would use pairs of numbers from the random-number table, with numbers "01-07" corresponding to get well, numbers "08-12" corresponding to "not get well", and all other numbers omitted. (If you wish to save time, you can work out a system that uses more numbers and skips fewer, but that is up to you.) Designate the first six subjects "pill" and the next six subjects "placebo".

The specific procedure might be as follows:

Step 1. "01-07" = get well, "08-12" = do not get well

Step 2. Select two groups, A and B, each with six random numbers from "01" to "12".

Step 3. Record how many "get well" in each group.

Step 4. Subtract the result in group A from that in group B (the difference may be negative).

Step 5. Repeat steps 1-4 perhaps 100 times.

Step 6. Compute the proportion of trials in which the pill does better by three or more cases. In the trials shown in Table 7-3, in three cases (12 percent) the difference between the randomly-drawn groups is three cases or greater. Apparently it is <u>somewhat</u> unusual -- it happens 12% of the time -- for this

155

universe to generate "pill" samples in which the number of recoveries exceeds the number in the "placebo" samples by three or more. Therefore the answer to the scientific question, based on these samples, is that there is some reason to think that the medicine does have a favorable effect. But the investigator might sensibly await more data before reaching a firm conclusion about the pill's efficiency, given the 7 to 1 odds (12 percent probability).

Table 7-4 Results of 25 Random Trials for Probability "Cancer"			
Trial	Pill Cures	Placebo Cures	Difference
1	4	4	0
2	3	5	-2
3	4	3	1
4*	5	2	3
5	4	3	1
6	2	5	-3
7	4	4	0
8	4	5	-1
9	4	4	0
10*	5	2	3
11	4	5	-1
12	5	3	2
13	3	5	-2
14	3	2	1
15	3	4	-1
16	5	4	1
17*	6	3	3
18	4	5	-1
19	3	4	-1
20	2	3	-1
21	4	4	0
22	4	4	0
23	3	5	-2
24	3	3	0
25	3	3	0

*The total is 3 differences as great as 3 in favor of pill

Now for a RESAMPLING STATS solution using the program "Cancer". Again, the benchmark hypothesis is that pill P has no effect, and we ask how often, on this assumption, the results that were obtained from the actual test of the pill would occur by chance.

Since in the test 7 of 12 patients got well overall, the benchmark hypothesis assumes 7/12 to be the chances of any random patient being cured. We GENERATE two similar samples of 6 patients, both taken from the same universe. Letting the values "1" through "7" denote a patient who got well and "8-12" denote not getting well, we COUNT the number who got well in each sample. Then we SUBTRACT the number who got well in the "pill" sample from the number who got well in the "no-pill" sample, and SCORE the resulting difference for each trial in Z.

In the actual test, 3 more patients got well in the sample given the pill than in the sample not given the pill. We therefore check how many of the trials yield results where the difference between the sample given the pill and the sample not given the pill was greater than 2 (equal to or greater than 3). This result is the probability that the results derived from the actual test would be obtained from random samples drawn from a population which has a constant cure rate, pill or no pill.

Program "CANCER"

REPEAT 1000	Do 1000 experiments.
GENERATE 6 1,12 A	Randomly generate 6 numbers between 1 and 12. Let 1-7 = cure, 8-12 = no cure. This will be the "medicine" group.
GENERATE 6 1,12 B	Similarly for the "placebo" group.
COUNT A between 1 7 AA	Count the number of cures in the trial "medicine" group. ("Medicine" is in quotes because the vector A is an arbitrary random selection of our

experiment -- one we know has no medicinal value because the cure rate -7/12 - is the same as for the "placebo" experimental group.)

COUNT B between 1 7 BB	Count the number of cures in the trial "placebo" group.
SUBTRACT AA BB K	Subtract trial "placebo" cures from trial "medicine" cures.
SCORE K Z	Keep track of each trial result in Z.
END	End one experiment, go back and repeat until 1000 are complete, then proceed.
HISTOGRAM Z	Produce a histogram of the trial results.

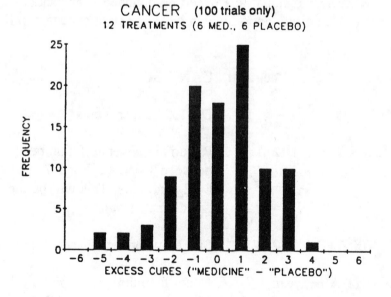

CANCER (100 trials only)
12 TREATMENTS (6 MED., 6 PLACEBO)

Recall our observed results: in the medicine group 3, more patients were cured than in the placebo group. From the histogram, we see that in only 11% of the chance draws did the trial "medicine" group do as well or better. The results seem to suggest that the medicine's performance is not due to chance, but by no means conclusively. Further study would probably be warranted. The following commands added to the above program will calculate this 11% proportion directly:

```
COUNT Z >= 3 L          Determine how often the
                        "medicine" group exceeded the
                        "placebo" group.

DIVIDE L 1000 LL        Convert to a proportion.

PRINT Z LL              Print the result.
```

This method is not the standard way of handling the problem; it is not even analogous to the standard analytic difference-of-proportions method. Though the method shown is quite direct and satisfactory, there are also many other resampling methods that one might construct to solve the same problem. By all means, invent your own statistics rather than simply trying to copy the methods described here; the examples given here only illustrate the process of inventing statistics rather than offering solutions for all classes of problems.

Example 7-5: Do Four Psychological Treatments Differ in Effectiveness? (Do Several Two-Outcome Samples Differ Among Themselves in Their Proportions? (Program "Delinquent")

Consider now, not two, but four, different psychological treatments designed to rehabilitate juvenile delinquents. Instead of a numerical test score, there is only a "yes" or a "no" answer as to whether the juvenile has been rehabilitated or has gotten into trouble again. Label the treatments P, R, S, and T, each of which is administered to a separate group of twenty juvenile delinquents. The number of rehabilitations per group has been: P, 17; R, 10; S, 10; T, 7. Is it improbable that all four groups come from the same universe?

This problem is like the placebo vs. cancer-cure problem, but now there are more than two samples. It is also like the four-sample irradiated-fruit flies example, except that in this case we are <u>not</u> asking whether any or some of the samples differ from a <u>given universe</u> (50-50 sex ratio in that case). Rather, we are now asking whether there are differences <u>among</u> the samples themselves. Please keep in mind that we are still dealing with two-outcome (yes-or-no, well-or-sick) problems. Later we shall take up problems that are similar except that the outcomes are "quantitative".

If all four groups come from the same universe, that universe has an estimated rehabilitation rate of 17/20 + 10/20 + 10/20 + 7/20 = 44/80 = 55/100 because the observed data <u>taken as a whole</u> constitute our best guess as to the nature of the universe from which they come -- <u>if</u> they all come from the same universe. (Please think this matter over a bit, because it is important and subtle. It may help you to notice the absence of any <u>other</u> information about the universe from which they have all come, if they have come from the same universe.)

Therefore, select twenty two-digit numbers for each group from the random-number table, marking "yes" for each number "1-55" and "no" for each number "56-100". Conduct a number of such trials. Then count the proportion of times that the difference between the highest and lowest groups is larger than the widest observed difference, that between P and T (17 - 7 = 10). In Table 7-5, none of the first six trials shows anywhere near as large a difference as the observed range of 10, suggesting that it would be rare for four treatments that are "really" similar to show so great a difference. There is thus reason to believe that P and T differ in their effects.

		Table 7-5			
	Results of Six Random Trials for Problem "Delinquents"				
Trial	P	R	S	T	Largest Minus Smallest
1	11	9	8	12	4
2	10	10	12	12	2
3	9	12	8	12	4
4	9	11	12	10	3
5	10	10	11	12	1
6	11	11	9	11	2

The strategy of the RESAMPLING STATS solution to "Delinquents" is similar to the strategy for previous problems in this chapter. The benchmark (null) hypothesis is that the treatments do not differ in their effects observed, and we estimate the probability that the observed results would occur by chance using the benchmark universe. The only new twist is that we must order the computer to find the groups with the highest and the lowest numbers of rehabilitations.

Using RESAMPLING STATS we GENERATE four "treatments," each represented by 20 numbers, each number randomly selected between 1 and 100. We let 1-55 = success, 56-100 = failure. Follow along in the program for the rest of the procedure:

Program "4TREAT1"

REPEAT 1000   Do 1000 trials

    GENERATE 20 1,100 A   The first treatment group, where 1-55 = success, 56-100 = failure

    GENERATE 20 1,100 B   The second group

GENERATE 20 1,100 C	The third group
GENERATE 20 1,100 D	The fourth group
COUNT A <=55 AA	Count the first group's successes
COUNT B <=55 BB	Same for second, third & fourth groups
COUNT C <=55 CC	
COUNT D <=55 DD	
SUBTRACT AA BB AB	Now find all the pairwise differences in successes among the groups
SUBTRACT AA CC AC	
SUBTRACT AA DD AD	
SUBTRACT BB CC BC	
SUBTRACT BB DD BD	
SUBTRACT CC DD CD	
CONCAT AB AC AD BC BD CD E	CONCATenate, or join, all the differences in a single vector E
ABS E F	Since we are interested only in the magnitude of the difference, not its direction, we take the ABSolute value of all the differences.
MAX F G	Find the largest of all the differences

```
SCORE G Z                  Keep score of the largest

END                        End a trial, go back and repeat until
                           all 1000 are complete.

COUNT Z >=10 K             How many of the trials yielded a
                           maximum difference greater than
                           the observed maximum difference?

DIVIDE K 1000 KK           Convert to a proportion

PRINT KK
```

In one run of the program, the experiments with randomly generated treatments from a common success rate of .55 produced differences in excess of the observed maximum difference (10) 1% of the time.

An alternative approach to this problem would be to deal with each result's departure from the mean, rather than the largest difference among the pairs. Once again, we want to deal with <u>absolute</u> departures, since we are interested only in magnitude of difference. We could take the absolute value of the differences, as above, but we will try something different here. <u>Squaring</u> the differences also renders them all positive, and this is a common approach in statistics.

The first step is to examine our data and calculate this measure: The mean is 11, the differences are 6, 1, 1, and 4, the squared differences are 36, 1, 1, and 16, and their sum is 54. Our experiment will be, as before, to constitute four groups of 20 at random from a universe with a 55% rehabilitation rate. We then calculate this same measure for the random groups. If it is frequently larger than 54, then we conclude that a uniform cure rate of 55% could easily have produced the observed results. The program that follows also GENERATES the four treatments by using a REPEAT loop, rather than spelling out the GENERATE command 4 times as above. In RESAMPLING STATS:

Program "4TREAT2"

REPEAT 1000	Do 1000 trials
REPEAT 4	Repeat the following steps 4 times to constitute 4 groups of 20 and count their rehabilitation rates.
GENERATE 20 1,100 A	Randomly generate 20 numbers between 1 and 100 and put them in A; let 1-55 = rehabilitation, 56-100 no rehab.
COUNT A between 1 55 B	Count the number of rehabs, put the result in B.
SCORE B W	Keep track of each of the 4 rehab rates.
END	End the procedure for one group of 20, go back and repeat until all 4 are done.
MEAN W X	Calculate the mean
SUBTRACT W X Y	Calculate the differences.
MULTIPLY Y Y YY	Square the differences.
SUM YY YYSUM	Sum the squared differences.
SCORE YYSUM Z	Keep track of the result for each trial.
CLEAR W	Erase the contents of W to prepare for the next trial.

END	End one experiment, go back and repeat until all 1000 are complete.
HISTOGRAM Z	Produce a histogram of trial results.

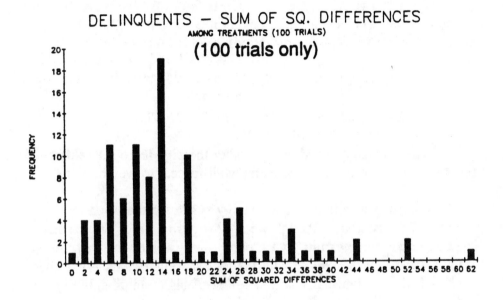

DELINQUENTS – SUM OF SQ. DIFFERENCES
AMONG TREATMENTS (100 TRIALS)
(100 trials only)

From this histogram, we see that in only 1% of the cases did our trial differences equal or exceed 54, confirming our conclusion that this is an unusual result. We can have RESAMPLING STATS calculate this proportion:

COUNT Z >= 54 K	Determine how many trials produced differences as great as those observed.
DIVIDE K 1000 KK	Convert to a proportion.
PRINT KK	Print the results.

The conventional way to approach this problem would be with what is known as a "chi-square test".

Example 7-6: Is One Pig Ration More Effective Than the Other? (Testing For a Difference in Means With a Two-by-Two Classification.) (Program "Pigs1")

Each of two new types of ration is fed to twelve pigs. A farmer wants to know whether ration A or ration B is better. [2] The weight gains in pounds for pigs fed on rations A and B are

A: 31, 34, 29, 26, 32, 35, 38, 34, 31, 29, 32, 31

B: 26, 24, 28, 29, 30, 29, 31, 29, 32, 26, 28, 32

The statistical question is whether the pigs fed on the different rations come from the same universe with respect to weight gains.

One approach is to use a strategy similar to that used in Example 7-5 just above, though we now require a bit of arbitrariness. We can divide the pigs into two groups -- the twelve with the highest weight gains, and the twelve with the lowest weight gains -- and then check whether an unusually large number of high-weight-gain pigs were fed on one or the other of the rations.

We can make this test by ordering and grouping the twenty-four pigs:

High-weight group: 38 (ration A), 35 (A), 34 (A), 34 (A), 32 (B), 32 (A), 32 (A), 32 (B), 31 (A), 31 (B), 31 (A), 31 (A)

Low-weight group: 30 (B), 29 (A), 29 (A), 29 (B), 29 (B), 29 (B), 28 (B), 28 (B), 26 (A), 26 (B), 26 (B), 24 (B).

Among the twelve high-gain pigs, nine were fed on ration A. We ask: Is this further from an even split than we are likely to get by chance?

Take twelve red and twelve black cards, shuffle them, and deal out twelve cards. Count the proportion of the hands in which one ration comes up nine or more times in the first twelve cards, to reflect ration A's appearance nine times among the highest twelve weight gains. More specifically:

Step 1. Constitute a deck of twelve red and twelve black cards, and shuffle.

Step 2. Deal out twelve cards, count the number red, and record "yes" if there are nine or more of <u>either</u> red or black.

Step 3. Repeat step 2 perhaps fifty times.

Step 4. Compute the proportion "yes". This proportion estimates the probability sought.

Table 7-6 shows the results of fifty trials. In three (marked by asterisks) of the fifty (6 percent, that is, of the trials) there were nine or more either red or black cards in the first twelve cards. Again the results suggest that it would be <u>slightly unusual</u> for the results to favor one ration or the other so strongly just by chance if they come from the same universe.

Trial	Black	Red	Trial	Black	Red	Trial	Black	Red
				Table 7-6				
			RESULTS OF FIFTY RANDOM TRIALS FOR PROBLEM "PIGS1"					
1	7	5	19	5	7	37	6	6
2	7	5	20	5	7	38	5	7
3	6	6	21	4	8	39	7	5
4	6	6	*22	9	3	40	5	7
5	6	6	23	7	5	41	6	6
6	4	8	24	5	7	42	4	8
7	6	6	25	5	7	43	7	5
8	6	6	26	7	5	44	5	7
9	5	7	27	6	6	45	8	4
10	8	4	*28	9	3	46	5	7
11	6	6	29	7	5	47	5	7
12	7	5	30	7	5	48	6	6
13	8	4	31	8	4	49	6	6
14	5	7	*32	3	9	50	6	6
15	6	6	33	5	7			
16	7	5	34	6	6			
17	8	4	35	5	7			
18	8	4	36	5	7			

*A trial with nine or more red cards, or 9 or more black cards.

Now a RESAMPLING STATS procedure to answer the question.

In the actual experiment, 9 of the 12 pigs who were fed ration A also were in the top half of weight gains. How likely is it that one group of 12 randomly-chosen pigs would contain 9 of the 12 top weight gainers?

The NUMBERS statement creates an array of numbers "1" through "24", which will represent the rankings of weight gains for each of the 24 pigs. We REPEAT the following procedure for 1000 trials. First we SHUFFLE the elements of array A so that the rank numbers for weight gains are randomized and placed in array B. We then TAKE the first 12 elements of B and place them in C; this represents the rankings of a randomly-selected group of 12 pigs. We next COUNT in C the number of pigs whose rankings for weight gain were in the top half -- that is, a rank of less than 13. We SCORE that number and END the loop.

Since we did not know beforehand the direction of the effect of ration A on weight gain, we want to count the times that <u>either more than 8</u> of the random selection of 12 pigs were in the top half of the rankings, <u>or that fewer than 4</u> of these pigs were in the top half of the weight gain rankings -- (The latter is the same as counting the number of times that more than 8 of the 12 <u>non-selected</u> random pigs were in the top half in weight gain.)

We do so with the final two COUNT statements. By adding the two results J and K together, we have the number of times out of 1000 that differences in weight gains in two groups as dramatic as those obtained in the actual experiment would occur by chance.

Program "PIGS1"

NUMBERS 1,24 A   Constitute the set of the weight gain rank orders. A is now a vector consisting of the numbers 1 - 24, in that order.

REPEAT 1000   Do the following experiment 1000 times.

SHUFFLE A B   Shuffle the ranks of the weight gains, put the shuffled ranks in B.

TAKE B 1,12 C   Take the first 12 ranks, put them in C.

COUNT C <= 12 D   Determine how many of these randomly
                   selected 12 ranks are less than 12 (i.e. 1-
                   12), put that result in D.

SCORE D Z   Keep track of each trial result in Z.

END   End one experiment, go back and repeat
                   until 1000 trials are complete.

HISTOGRAM Z   Produce a histogram of the trial results.

PIGS1: RANDOM SELECTION OF 12
WEIGHT GAINS (24 PIGS, 100 TRIALS)

We see from the histogram that, in 4% of the trials, either more than 8 or fewer than 4 top half ranks (1-12) made it into the random group of twelve that we selected. RESAMPLING STATS will calculate this for us as follows:

COUNT Z >= 9 J	Determine how many of the trials yielded 9 or more top ranks.
COUNT Z <= 3 K	Determine how many trials yielded 3 or fewer of the top ranks.
ADD J K L	Add the two together.
DIVIDE L 1000 LL	Convert to a proportion.
PRINT LL	Print the results.

The decisions that are warranted on the basis of the estimates depend upon one's purpose. If writing a scientific paper on the merits of ration A is the ultimate purpose, it would be sensible to test another batch of pigs to get further evidence. (Or you could proceed to employ another sort of test for a slightly more precise evaluation.) But if the goal is a decision on which type of ration to buy for a small farm and they are the same price, just go ahead and buy ration A because, even if it is no better than ration B, you have strong evidence that it is no worse.

Example 7-7: The Pig Rations Again, But Comparing Pairs of Pigs (Paired-Comparison Test) (Program "Pigs2")

To illustrate how several procedures can reasonably be used for a given problem, here is another way to decide whether ration A is "really" better: We can assume that the order of the pig scores listed within each ration group is random -- perhaps the order of the stalls the pigs were kept in, or their alphabetical-name order, or any other random order not related to their weights. Then match the first pig on ration A with the first pig on ration B, and also match the second pigs, the third

171

pigs, and so forth. Then count the number of matched pairs on which ration A does better. On nine of twelve pairings ration A does better, that is, 31.0 > 26.0, 34.0 > 24.0, and so forth.

Now we can ask: If the two rations are equally good, how often will one exceed the other nine or more times out of twelve? This is the same as asking how often either heads or tails will come up nine or more times in twelve tosses. (Because, as far as we know, either ration may be as good as or better than the other, this is a "two-tailed" test.)

Once we have decided to treat the problem in this manner, it is quite similar to Example 7-1 (the first fruit fly irradiation problem). We ask how likely it is that the outcome will be as far away as the observed outcome (9 "heads" of 12) from 6 of 12 (which is what we expect to get by chance in this case if the two rations are similar).

So we run perhaps fifty trials as in Table 7-7 where an asterisk denotes nine or more heads or tails.

Step 1. Let odd numbers equal "A better" and even numbers equal "B better".

Step 2. Examine 12 random digits and check whether 9 or more, or 3 or less, are odd. If so, record "yes", otherwise "no".

Step 3. Repeat step 2 fifty times.

Step 4. Compute the proportion "yes", which estimates the probability sought.

The results are shown in table 7-7.

	Table 7-7				
	RESULTS FROM FIFTY SIMULATION TRIALS OF THE PROBLEM "PIGS2"				
Trial	"Heads" or "Odds" (Ration A)	"Tails" or "Evens" (Ration B)	Trial	"Heads" or "Odds" (Ration A)	"Tails" or "Evens" (Ration B)
1	6	6	26	6	6
2	4	8	27	5	7
3	6	6	28	7	5
4	7	5	29	4	8
*5	3	9	30	6	6
6	5	7	*31	9	3
7	8	4	*32	2	10
8	6	6	33	7	5
9	7	5	34	5	7
*10	9	3	35	6	6
11	7	5	36	8	4
*12	3	9	37	6	6
13	5	7	38	4	8
14	6	6	39	5	7
15	6	6	40	8	4
16	8	4	41	5	7
17	5	7	42	6	6
*18	9	3	43	5	7

Trial	"Heads" or "Odds" (Ration A)	"Tails" or "Evens" (Ration B)	Trial	"Heads" or "Odds" (Ration A)	"Tails" or "Evens" (Ration B)
19	6	6	44	7	5
20	7	5	45	6	6
21	4	8	46	4	8
*22	10	2	47	5	7
23	6	6	48	5	7
24	5	7	49	8	4
*25	3	9	50	7	5

Table 7-7 (Continued)

*Denotes the occurrence of 9 or more heads or tails.

In eight of fifty trials, one or the other ration had nine or more tosses in its favor. Therefore, the probability is estimated to be .16 (eight of fifty) that samples this different would be generated by chance if the samples came from the same universe.

Now for RESAMPLING STATS. "Pigs2" is different from "Pigs1" in that it compares the weight-gain results of <u>pairs</u> of pigs, instead of simply looking at the <u>rankings</u> for weight gains.

The key to "Pigs2" is the GENERATE statement. If we assume that ration A does not have an effect on weight gain (the "benchmark" or "null" hypothesis), then the results of the actual experiment would be no different than if we randomly GENERATE numbers "1" and "2" and treat a "1" as a larger weight gain for the ration A pig, and a "2" as a larger weight gain for the ration B pig. Both events have a 50-50 chance of occurring for each pair of pigs, because if (the null hypothesis) the rations had no effect on weight gain, ration A pigs would have larger weight gains about fifty percent of the time. The next step is to COUNT the number of times that the weight gains of one group (call it the group fed with ration A) were larger than the weight gains of the other (call it the group fed with ration B). The complete program follows:

Program "PIGS2"

REPEAT 100	Do 100 trials
GENERATE 12 1,2 A	Generate randomly 12 1's and 2's, put them in A. This represents 12 "pairings" where 1 = ration A "wins", 2 = ration B = "wins."
COUNT A =1 B	Count the number of "pairings" where ration A won, put the result in B.
SCORE B Z	Keep track of the result in Z
END	End the trial, go back and repeat until all 100 trials are complete.
COUNT Z >= 9 J	Determine how often we got 9 or more "wins" for ration A.
COUNT Z <= 3 K	Determine how often we got 3 or fewer "wins" for ration A.
ADD J K L	Add the two together
DIVIDE L 100 LL	Convert to a proportion
PRINT LL	Print the result.

Notice how we proceeded in Examples 7-6 and 7-7. The data were originally quantitative. That is, we have weight gains in pounds for each pig. But for simplicity we classified the data into simpler counted-data formats. The first format (Example 7-6) was a rank order, from highest to lowest. The second format (Example 7-7) was simply

175

higher-lower, obtained by randomly pairing the observations (using alphabetical letter, or pig's stall number, or whatever was the cause of the order in which the data were presented to be random). Classifying the data in either of these ways loses some information and makes the subsequent tests somewhat cruder than more refined analysis could provide (as we shall see in the next chapter), but the loss of efficiency is not crucial in many such cases.

NOTES:

Technical note: Some of the tests introduced in this chapter are similar to standard nonparametric rank and sign tests. They differ less in the structure of the test statistic than in the way in which its significance is assessed (the comparison is to multiple simulations of a model based on the benchmark hypothesis, rather than to critical values calculated analytically).

[1]   If you are very knowledgeable, you may do some in-between figuring (with what is known as "Bayesian analysis"), but leave this alone unless you know well what you are doing.

[2]   The data for this example are based on W. J. Dixon and F. J. Massey (1969, p. 117), who offer an orthodox method of handling the problem with a t-test.

CHAPTER 8

THE STATISTICS OF HYPOTHESIS-TESTING WITH MEASURED DATA

PREVIEW

EXAMPLE 8-1: The Pig Rations Still Once More, Using Measured Data (Testing for the Difference Between Means of Two Equal-Sized Samples of Measured-Data Observations)

EXAMPLE 8-2: Is There a Difference in Liquor Prices Between State-Run and Privately-Run Systems? (Testing for Differences Between Means of Unequal-Sized Samples of Measured Data)

EXAMPLE 8-3: Differences Among Four Pig Rations (Test For Differences Among Means of More Than Two Samples of Measured Data)

PREVIEW

The previous chapter discussed testing a hypothesis with data that come to you in dichotomized (yes-no) form, or measured data in situations where it is convenient to dichotomize. Now we move on to hypothesis testing using measured data. Conventional statistical practice employs such devices as the "t-test" and "analysis of variance." In contrast, the resampling method does not differ greatly from what has been discussed in previous chapters.

Now let us deal with the pig-ration problem without converting
the quantitative into qualitative data, because a conversion always loses
information.

The term "lose information" can be understood intuitively.
Consider two sets of three sacks of corn. Set A includes sacks
containing, respectively, one pound, two pounds, and three pounds. Set
B includes sacks of one pound, two pounds, and a hundred pounds. If
we rank by weight, the two sets can no longer be distinguished. The
one-pound and two-pound sacks have ranks one and two in both cases,
and their relative places in their sets are the same. But if we know not
only that the one-pound sack is the smallest of its set and the three-
pound or hundred-pound sack is the largest, but also that the largest
sack is three pounds (or a hundred pounds), we have more information
about a set than if we only know the ranks of its sacks.

Rank data are also known as "ordinal" data; measured data --
say, in pounds -- are known as "cardinal" data. Converting from
cardinal (measured) to ordinal (ranked) data loses information, but it
may increase convenience and therefore be worth doing sometimes.

We begin a measured-data approach by noting that if the two pig
rations are the same, then each of the observed weight gains came from
the same benchmark universe. This is the basic tactic in our statistical
strategy. That is, if the two rations came from the same universe, our
best guess about the composition of the universe is that it is composed
of weight gains just like the twenty-four we have observed, because that
is all the information that we have about the universe. Since ours is (by
definition) a sample from an infinite (or at least, a very large) universe
of possible weight gains, we assume that there are many weight gains in
the universe just like the ones we have observed, in the same proportion
as we have observed them. For example, we assume that 2/24 of the
universe is composed of 34-pound weight gains, as seen in Figure 8-1:

Figure 8-1

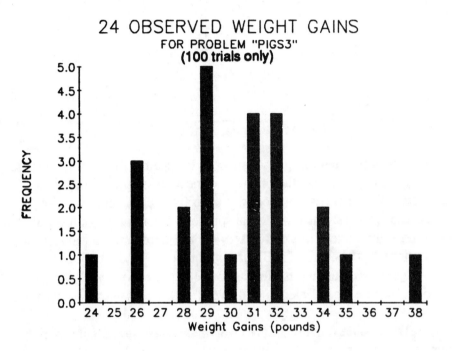

24 OBSERVED WEIGHT GAINS
FOR PROBLEM "PIGS3"
(100 trials only)

We recognize, of course, that weight gains other than the exact ones we observed certainly would occur in repeated experiments. And if we thought it reasonable to do so, we could assume that the "distribution" of the weight gains would follow a regular "smooth" shape such as Figure 8-2. But deciding just how to draw Figure 8-2 from the data in Figure 8-1 requires that we make arbitrary assumptions about unknown conditions. And if we were to draw Figure 8-2 in a form that would be sufficiently regular for conventional mathematical analysis, we might have to make some <u>very strong</u> assumptions going far beyond the observed data.

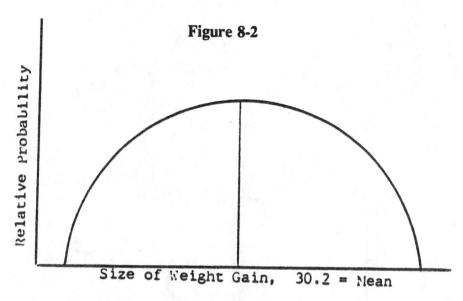

Figure 8-2

Relative Probability (vertical axis)

Size of Weight Gain, 30.2 = Mean

Drawing a smooth curve such as Figure 8-2 from the raw data in Figure 8-1 might be satisfactory -- if done with wisdom and good judgment. But there is no necessity to draw such a smooth curve, in this case or in most cases. We can proceed by assuming simply that the benchmark universe -- the universe we shall compare our samples to, conventionally called the "null" or "hypothetical" universe -- is composed only of elements similar to the observations we have in hand. We thereby lose no efficiency and avoid making unsound assumptions.

To execute our procedure, we write down each of the twenty-four weight gains on a blank index card. We then have one card each for 31, 34, 29, 26, and so on. Shuffle the twenty-four cards thoroughly, and pick one card. Record the weight gain, and replace the card. (Recall that we are treating the weight gains as if they come from an infinite universe - that is, as if the probability of selecting any amount as the same no matter which others are selected randomly. Another way to say this is to state that each selection is independent of each other selection. If we did not replace the card before selecting the next weight gain, the selections would no longer be independent. See Chapter 4 for further discussion of this issue.) Repeat this process until you have made two sets of 12 observations. Call the first hand "ration A" and the second hand "ration B." Determine the average weight gain for the two hands, and record it as in Table 8-1. Repeat this procedure many times.

In operational steps:

Step 1. Write down each observed weight gain on a card, e.g. 31, 34, 29...

Step 2. Shuffle and deal a card.

Step 3. Record the weight and replace the card.

Step 4. Repeat steps 2 and 3 eleven more times; call this group A.

Step 5. Repeat steps 2-3 another twelve times; call this group B.

Step 6. Calculate the mean weight gain of each group.

Step 7. Subtract the mean of group A from the mean of group B and record. If larger (more positive) than 3.16 (the difference between the observed means) or more negative than -3.16, record "more." Otherwise record "less."

Step 8. Repeat this procedure fifty times, and calculate the proportion "more." This estimates the probability sought.

In none of the first ten trials did the difference in the means of the random hands exceed the observed difference (3.16) pounds, in the top line in the table) between rations A and B. (The difference between group totals tells the same story and is faster, requiring no division calculations.)

Ordinarily I would quit making trials at such a point, confident that a difference in means as great as observed is not likely to happen by chance. (Using the quick multiplication rule described in Chapter 4, we can estimate the probability of such an occurrence happening by chance as $1/2 \times 1/2 \times 1/2 \ldots = (1/2)^{10} = 1/1024 \approx .001 = .1\%$, a small chance indeed.) Nevertheless, let us press on to do 50 trials.

Table 8-1
Results of Fifty Random Samples for the Problem "PIGS3"

	Mean of First Twelve Observations (First Hand)	Mean of Second Twelve Observations (Second Hand)	Difference	Greater or Less Than Observed Difference
Actually Observed	382/12=31.83	344/12=28.67	3.16	
Trial				
1	368/12=30.67	357/12=29.75	.87	Less
2	364/12=30.33	361/12=30.08	.25	"
3	352/12=29.33	373/12=31.08	(1.75)	"
4	378/12=31.50	347/12=28.92	2.58	"
5	365/12=30.42	360/12=30.00	.42	"
6	352/12=29.33	373/12=31.08	(1.75)	"
7	355/12=29.58	370/12=30.83	(1.25)	"
8	366/12=30.50	359/12=29.92	.58	"
9	360/12=30.00	365/12=30.42	(.42)	"
10	355/12=29.58	370/12=30.83	(1.25)	"
11	359/12=29.92	366/12=30.50	(.58)	"
12	369/12=30.75	356/12=29.67	1.08	"
13	360/12=30.00	365/12=30.42	(.42)	"
14	377/12=31.42	348/12=29.00	2.42	"
15	365/12=30.42	360/12=30.00	.42	"
16	364/12=30.33	361/12=30.08	.25	"
17	363/12=30.25	362/12=30.17	.08	"
18	365/12=30.42	360/12=30.00	.42	"
19	369/12=30.75	356/12=29.67	1.08	"
20	369/12=30.75	356/12=29.67	1.08	"
21	369/12=30.75	356/12=29.67	1.08	"
22	364/12=30.33	361/12=30.08	.25	"

182

Table 8-1 (Continued)

Trial	Mean of First Twelve Observations (First Hand)	Mean of Second Twelve Observations (Second Hand)	Difference	Greater or Less Than Observed Difference
23	363/12=30.25	362/12=30.17	.08	"
24	363/12=30.25	362/12=30.17	.08	"
25	364/12=30.33	361/12=30.08	.25	"
26	359/12=29.92	366/12=30.50	(.58)	"
27	362/12=30.17	363/12=30.25	(.08)	"
28	362/12=30.17	363/12=30.25	(.08)	"
29	373/12=31.08	352/12=29.33	1.75	"
30	367/12=30.58	358/12=29.83	.75	"
31	376/12=31.33	349/12=29.08	2.25	"
32	365/12=30.42	360/12=30.00	.42	"
33	357/12=29.75	368/12=30.67	(1.42)	"
34	349/12=29.08	376/12=31.33	2.25	"
35	356/12=29.67	396/12=30.75	(1.08)	"
36	359/12=29.92	366/12=30.50	(.58)	"
37	372/12=31.00	353/12=29.42	1.58	"
38	368/12=30.67	357/12=29.75	.92	"
39	344/12=28.67	382/12=31.81	(3.16)	Equal
40	365/12=30.42	360/12=30.00	.42	Less
41	375/12=31.25	350/12=29.17	2.08	"
42	353/12=29.42	372/12=31.00	(1.58)	"
43	357/12=29.75	368/12=30.67	(.92)	"
44	363/12=30.25	362/12=30.17	.08	"
45	353/12=29.42	372/12=31.00	(1.58)	"
46	354/12=29.50	371/12=30.92	(1.42)	"
47	353/12=29.42	372/12=31.00	(1.58)	"

48	366/12=30.50	350/12=29.92	.58	"
49	364/12=30.53	361/12=30.08	.25	"
50	370/12=30.83	355/12=29.58	1.25	"

Table 8-1 shows fifty trials of which only one (the thirty-ninth) is as "far out" as the observed samples. These data give us an estimate of the probability that, if the two rations come from the same universe, a difference this great or greater would occur just by chance. (Compare this estimate with the probability of roughly 99 percent estimated with the conventional t test, that is, a significance level of 1 percent.) On the average, the test described in this section yields a significance level as high as such mathematical-probability tests as the t test -- that is, it is just as efficient -- though the tests described in Examples 7-5 and 7-6 are likely to be less efficient because they convert measured data to ranked or classified data. [1]

This example also illustrates how the dispersion within samples affects the difficulty of finding out whether the samples differ from each other. For example, the average weight gain for ration A was 32 pounds, versus 29 pounds for ration B. If all the ration A-fed pigs had gained weight within a range of say 29.9 and 30.1 pounds, and if all the ration B-fed pigs had gained weight within a range of 28.9 and 29.1 pounds -- that is, if the highest weight gain in ration B had been lower than the lowest weight gain in ration A -- then there would be no question that ration A is better, and even fewer observations would have made this point clear. Variation (dispersion) is thus of great importance in statistics and in the social sciences. The larger the dispersion among the observations within the samples, the larger the sample size necessary to make a conclusive comparison between two groups or reliable estimates of summarization statistics. (The dispersion might be measured by the mean absolute deviation (the average absolute difference between the mean and the individual observations, treating both plus and minus differences as positive), the variance (the average squared difference between the mean and the observations), the standard deviation (the square root of the variance), the range (the difference between the smallest and largest observations), or some other device.)

If you are performing your tests by hand rather than using a computer, you might prefer to work with the median instead of the mean, for the median requires less computation. (The median also has the advantage of being less influenced by a single far-out observation which might be quite atypical; all measures have their special advantages and disadvantages.) Simply compare the difference in medians of the twelve-pig resamples to the difference in medians of the actual samples, just as was done with the means. The only operational difference is to substitute the word "median" for the word "mean" in the steps listed above. You may need a somewhat larger number of trials when working with medians, however, for they tend to be less precise than means.

The RESAMPLING STATS program compares the difference in the sums of the weight gains for the actual pigs against the difference resulting from two randomly-chosen groups of pigs, but using the same numerical weight gains of individual pigs as were obtained in the actual experiment. If the differences in average (actually, computed as a total) weight gains of the randomly ordered groups are rarely as large as the difference in weight gains from the actual sets of pigs fed ration A-alpha and ration B-beta, then we can conclude that the rations do make a difference in pigs' weight gains.

Note first that group A pigs gained a total of 382 pounds; group B a total of 344 pounds -- 38 fewer. To minimize computations, we will deal with totals like these, not averages.

First we construct vectors A and B of the weight gains of the pigs fed with the two rations. Then we combine the two vectors into one long vector and select two groups of 12 randomly and with replacement (the two SAMPLE commands). We SUM the weight gains for the two resamples, and calculate the difference. We keep SCORE of those differences, graph them on a HISTOGRAM, and see how many times resample A exceeded resample B by at least 38 pounds, or vice versa (we are testing whether the two are different, not whether ration A produces larger weight gains).

Program "PIGS3"

NUMBERS (31 34 29 26 32 35 38 34 31 29 32 31) A

                Record group A's weight gains.

NUMBERS (26 24 28 29 30 29 31 29 32 26 28 32) B

                Record group B's weight gains.

CONCAT A B C   Combine A and B together in one long vector.

REPEAT 1000   Do 1000 experiments.

   SAMPLE 12 C D   Take a "resample" of 12 with replacement from C and put it in D.

   SAMPLE 12 C E   Take another "resample".

   SUM D DD   Sum the first "resample".

   SUM E EE   Sum the second "resample".

   SUBTRACT DD EE F   Calculate the difference between the two resamples.

   SCORE F Z   Keep track of each trial result.

END   End one experiment, go back and repeat until all trials are complete, then proceed.

HISTOGRAM Z   Produce a histogram of trial results.

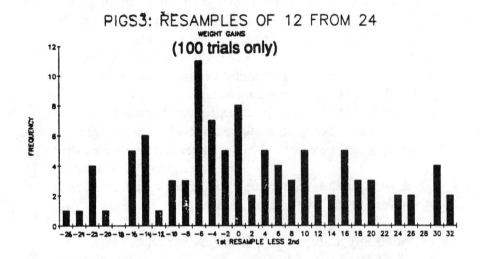

PIGS3: RESAMPLES OF 12 FROM 24
WEIGHT GAINS
(100 trials only)

FREQUENCY

1st RESAMPLE LESS 2nd

From this histogram we see that none of the trials produced a difference between groups as large as that observed (or larger). RESAMPLING STATS will calculate this for us with the following commands:

COUNT Z >= 38 K   Determine how many of the trials produced a difference between resamples >= 38.

COUNT Z <= -38 L   Likewise for a difference of -38.

ADD K L M   Add the two together.

DIVIDE M 1000 MM   Convert to a proportion.

PRINT MM   Print the result.

187

The pig-ration example dealt with equal numbers of pigs in each litter. The technique demonstrated in Example 8-1 is quite flexible, however, and can be used with unequal-sized samples.

In the 1960s I studied the price of liquor in the sixteen "monopoly" states (where the state government owns the retail liquor stores) compared to the twenty-six states in which retail liquor stores are privately owned. (Some states were omitted for technical reasons. The situation and the price pattern has changed radically since then.)

These were the representative 1961 prices of a fifth of Seagram 7 Crown whiskey in the two sets of states:

16 monopoly states: $4.65, $4.55, $4.11, $4.15, $4.20,$4.55, $3.80, $4.00, $4.19, $4.75, $4.74, $4.50, $4.10,$4.00, $5.05, $4.20. Mean: $4.35

26 private-ownership states: $4.82, $5.29, $4.89, $4.95, $4.55, $4.90, $5.25, $5.30, $4.29, $4.85, $4.54,$4.75, $4.85, $4.85, $4.50, $4.75, $4.79, $4.85, $4.79, $4.95, $4.95, $4.75, $5.20, $5.10, $4.80, $4.29. Mean: $4.84

The economic question that underlay the investigation - having both theoretical and policy ramifications - is as follows: Does state ownership affect prices? The empirical question is whether the prices in the two sets of states were systematically different. In statistical terms, we wish to test the hypothesis that there was a difference between the groups of states related to their mode of liquor distribution, or whether instead the observed $.49 differential in means might well have occurred by happenstance. In other words, we want to know whether the two sub-groups of states differed systematically in their liquor prices, or whether the observed pattern could well have been produced by chance variability.

At first I used a resampling permutation test as follows: Assuming that the entire universe of possible prices consists of the set of events that were observed, because that is all the information available about the universe, I wrote each of the forty-two observed state prices on a separate card. The shuffled deck simulated a situation in which each state has an equal chance for each price.

On the "null hypothesis" that the two groups' prices do <u>not</u> reflect different price-setting mechanisms, but rather differ only by chance, I then examined how often that simulated universe stochastically produces groups with results as different as observed in 1961. I repeatedly dealt groups of 16 and 26 cards, without replacing the cards, to simulate hypothetical monopoly-state and private-state samples, each time calculating the difference in mean prices.

The probability that the benchmark null-hypothesis universe would produce a difference between groups as large or larger than observed in 1961 is estimated by how frequently the mean of the group of randomly-chosen sixteen prices from the simulated state-ownership universe is less than (or equal to) the mean of the actual sixteen state-ownership prices. If the simulated difference between the randomly-chosen groups was frequently equal to or greater than observed in 1961, one would not conclude that the observed difference was due to the type of retailing system because it could well have been due to chance variation.

The computer program "LIQUOR" using the language RESAMPLING STATS performs the operations described above:

Program "LIQUOR"

NUMBERS (482 529 489 495 455 490 525 530 429 485 454 475 485 485 450 475 479 485 479 495 495 475 520 510 480 429) A

> Record the private enterprise state prices.

NUMBERS (465 455 411 415 420 455 380 400 419 475 474 450 410 400 505 420) B

> Record state monopoly prices.

CONCAT A B C

> Combine all the prices together.

REPEAT 1000

> Repeat the experiment 1000 times.

    SHUFFLE C D

> Shuffle the prices.

    TAKE D 1,26 E

> Take the first 26 prices from D, put them in E. This will represent our pseudo private enterprise group.

    TAKE D 27,42 F

> Take the remaining 16 prices from D, put them in F. This is our pseudo monopoly group.

    MEAN E EE

> Calculate the means.

    MEAN F FF

    SUBTRACT EE FF G

> Take the pseudo-private average and subtract the pseudo-monopoly average; put the result in G.

    SCORE G Z

> Keep track of each trial result in Z.

END

> End the experiment, go back and repeat until 1000 trials are complete.

Produce a histogram of the results.

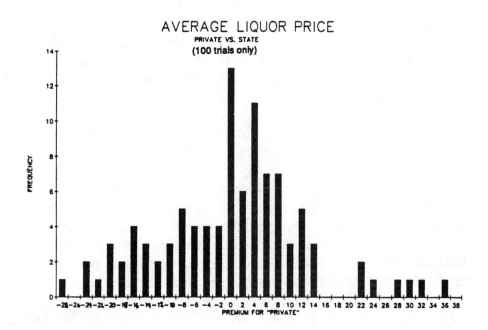

From the histogram, we see that in none of the cases did the pseudo-private price exceed the pseudo-monopoly price by 49 cents or more. We conclude that the observed result is likely not due to chance variation. We can use RESAMPLING STATS to calculate this proportion directly:

COUNT Z >= 49 K	Determine how many trials produced a pseudo-private group at least 49 cents more expensive than the pseudo-monopoly group.
DIVIDE K 1000 KK	Convert to a proportion.
PRINT K	Print the result.

The results shown - not even one "success" in 1000 trials - imply a very small probability that two groups with mean prices as different as were observed would happen by chance if drawn from the universe of 42 observed prices. So we "reject the null hypothesis" and instead find persuasive the proposition that the type of liquor distribution system influences the prices that consumers pay. As I shall discuss later, the logical framework of this resampling version of the permutation test differs greatly from the formulaic version, which would have required heavy computation. The standard conventional alternative would be a Student's t-test, in which the user simply plugs into an unintuitive formula and table. And because of the unequal numbers of cases and unequal dispersions in the two samples, an appropriate t test is far from obvious, whereas resampling is not made more difficult by such realistic complications.

Recently I have concluded that a bootstrap-type test has better theoretical justification than a permutation test in this case, though the two reach almost identical results with a sample this large. The following discussion of which is most appropriate brings out the underlying natures of the two approaches, and illustrates how resampling raises issues which tend to be buried amidst the technical complexity of the formulaic methods, and hence are seldom discussed in print.

Imagine a class of 42 students, 16 men and 26 women who come into the room and sit in 42 fixed seats. We measure the distance of each seat to the lecturer, and assign each a rank. The women sit in ranks 1-5, 7-20, etc., and the men in ranks 6, 22, 25-26, etc. You ask: Is there a relationship between sex and ranked distance from the front? Here the permutation procedure that resamples without replacement - as used above with the state liquor prices - quite clearly is appropriate.

Now, how about if we work with actual distances from the front? If there are only 42 seats and they are fixed, the permutation test and sampling without replacement again is appropriate. But how about if seats are movable?

Consider the possible situation in which one student can choose position without reference to others. That is, if the seats are movable, it is not only imaginable that A would be sitting where B now is, with B in A's present seat - as was the case with the fixed chairs - but A could now change distance from the lecturer while all the others remain as they are. Sampling with replacement now is appropriate. (To use a technical term, the cardinal data provide more actual degrees of freedom - more information - than do the ranks).

Note that (as with the liquor prices) the seat distances do not comprise an infinite population. Rather, we are inquiring whether a) the universe should be considered limited to a given number of elements, or b) could be considered expandable without change in the probabilities; the latter is a useful definition of "sampling with replacement".

As of 1992, the U.S. state liquor systems seem to me to resemble a non-fixed universe (like non-fixed chairs) even though the actual number of states is presently fixed. The question the research asked was whether the liquor system affects the price of liquor. We can imagine another state being admitted to the union, or one of the existing states changing its system, and pondering how the choice of system will affect the price. And there is no reason to believe that (at least in the short run) the newly-made choice of system would affect the other states' pricing; hence it makes sense to sample with replacement (and use the bootstrap) even though the number of states clearly is not infinite or greatly expandable.

In short, the presence of interaction - a change in one entity causing another entity also to change - implies a finite universe composed of those elements, and use of a permutation test. Conversely, when one entity can change independently, an infinite universe and sampling with replacement with a bootstrap test is indicated.

A program to handle the liquor problem with an infinite-universe bootstrap distribution simply substitutes the random sampling command SAMPLE for the TAKE command in the program "LIQUOR". The results of the new test are indistinguishable from those in "LIQUOR".

In Examples 7-1 and 7-4 we investigated whether or not the results shown by a <u>single</u> sample are sufficiently different from a null (benchmark) hypothesis so that the sample is unlikely to have come from the null-hypothesis benchmark universe. In Examples 7-6, 7-7, and 8-1 we then investigated whether or not the results shown by <u>two</u> samples suggest that both had come from the <u>same</u> universe, a universe that was assumed to be the composite of the two samples. Now as in Example 7-2 we investigate whether or not <u>several</u> samples come from the same universe, except that now we work with measured data rather than with counted data.

If one experiments with each of 100 different pig rations on twelve pigs, some of the rations will show much better results than will others <u>just by chance</u>, just as one family in sixteen is likely to have the very "high" number of 4 daughters in its first four children. Therefore, it is wrong reasoning to try out the 100 pig rations, select the ration that shows the best results, and then compare it statistically with the average (sum) of all the other rations (or worse, with the poorest ration). With such a procedure and enough samples, you will surely find one (or more) that seems very atypical statistically. A bridge hand with 12 or 13 spades seems very atypical, too, but if you deal enough bridge hands you will sooner or later get one with 12 or 13 spades -- as a purely chance phenomenon, dealt randomly from a standard deck. Therefore we need a test that prevents our falling into such traps. Such a test usually operates by taking into account the differences among <u>all</u> the rations that were tried.

The method of Example 8-1 can be extended to handle this problem. Assume that <u>four</u> rations were each tested on twelve pigs. The weight gains in pounds for the pigs fed on rations A and B were as before. For rations C and D the weight gains were:

Ration C: 30, 30, 32, 31, 29, 27, 25, 30, 31, 32, 34, 33

Ration D: 32, 25, 31, 26, 32, 27, 28, 29, 29, 28, 23, 25

Now construct a benchmark universe of <u>forty-eight</u> index cards, one for each weight gain. Then deal out sets of four hands randomly.

More specifically:

Step 1. Constitute a universe of the forty-eight observed weight gains in the four samples, writing the weight gains on cards.

Step 2. Draw four groups of twelve weight gains, with replacement, since we are drawing from a hypothesized infinite universe in which consecutive draws are independent. Determine whether the difference between the lowest and highest group means is as large or larger than the observed difference. If so write "yes," otherwise "no."

Step 3. Repeat step 2 fifty times.

Step 4. Count the trials in which the differences between the simulated groups with the highest and lowest means are not as large as the differences between the means of the highest and lowest observed samples. The proportion of such trials to the total number of trials is the probability that all four samples do not come from the same universe.

The problem "Pigs4," as handled by the steps given above, is thoroughly similar to the way we handled Example 7-5, except that the data are measured (in pounds of weight gain) rather than simply counted (the number of rehabilitations).

Instead of working through a program for the procedure outlined above, let us consider a different approach to the problem, -- computing the difference between each <u>pair</u> of rations, six differences in all, converting all minus (-) signs to (+) differences. Then <u>total</u> the six differences, and compare the total with the sum of the six differences in the <u>observed</u> sample. The proportion of times that the observed sample sum is not exceeded by the sum of the differences in the trials is the probability that the observed samples do not come from the same universe - - in this case. [4]

One naturally wonders whether this latter approach is better than working with the range, as discussed above. It would seem obvious that using the information contained in all four samples should increase the precision of the estimate. And indeed it is so, as you can confirm for yourself by comparing the results of the two approaches. But in the long run, the estimate provided by the two approaches would be much the same. That is, there is no reason to think that one or another of the estimates is biased. However, successive samples from the population would steady down faster to the true value using the four-group-based estimate than would using the range. That is, the four-group-based estimate would require a smaller sample of pigs.

Is there reason to prefer one or the other approach from the point of view of some decision that might be made? One might think that the range approach throws light on which one of the rations is best in a way that the four-group-based approach does not. But this is not correct. Both approaches answer the question and only this question: Are the results from the four rations likely to have resulted from the same "universe" of weight gains or not? If one wants to know whether the best ration is similar to, say, all the other three, the appropriate approach would be a two-sample approach similar to various two-sample examples discussed earlier. (It would be still another question to ask whether the best ration is different from the worst. One would then use a procedure different from either of those discussed above.)

If the rations cost the same, one would not need even a two-sample analysis to decide which ration to feed. Feed the one whose results are best in the experiment, without bothering to ask whether it is "really" the best; you can't go wrong as long as it doesn't cost more to use it. (One could inquire about the probability that the ration yielding the best results in the experiment would attain those results by chance even if it was worse than the others by some stipulated amount, but pursuing that line of thought may be left to the student as an exercise.)

In the problem "PIGS4," w   'nt a measure of how the groups differ. The obvious first step is to a   the total weight gains for each group: 382, 344, 364, 335. The next step is to calculate the differences between all the possible combinations of groups: 382-344=38, 382-364=18, 382-335=47, 344-364= -20, 344-335=9, 364-335=29.

Here we have a choice. We could work with the absolute differences -- that is, the results of the subtractions -- treating each result as a positive number even if it is negative. When we begin our RESAMPLING STATS simulations, however, this will require several statements for each pair -- a subtraction and then a comparison done with an IF statement, a comparison, a MOVE statement, and END. Both because this requires so many statements, and also because we have seen this approach before and therefore can show another approach, we try another device. Instead of working with the absolute differences, we square each difference, and then SUM the squares. An advantage of working with the squares is that they are positive -- a negative number squared is positive -- which is convenient. Additionally, conventional statistics works mainly with squared quantities, and therefore it is worth getting familiar with that point of view. The squared differences in this case add up to 5299.

Using RESAMPLING STATS, we shuffle all the weight gains together, select four random groups, and determine whether the squared differences in the resample exceed 5299. If they do so with regularity, then we conclude that the observed differences could easily have occurred by chance.

With the CONCAT command, we string the four vectors into a single vector. After SHUFFLEing the 48-pig weight-gain vector G into H, we TAKE four randomized samples. And we compute the squared differences between the pairs of groups and SUM the squared differences just as we did above for the observed groups.

Last, we examine how often the simulated-trials data produce differences among the groups as large as (or larger than) the actually observed data - 5299.

Program "PIGS4"

NUMBERS (34 29 26 32 35 38 31 34 30 29 32 31) A

NUMBERS (26 24 28 29 30 29 32 26 31 29 32 28) B

NUMBERS (30 30 32 31 29 27 25 30 31 32 34 33) C

NUMBERS (32 25 31 26 32 27 28 29 29 28 23 25) D

	(Record the data for the 4 rations)
CONCAT A B C D G	Combine the four vectors into G.
REPEAT 1000	Do 1000 trials.
SHUFFLE G H	Shuffle all the weight gains.
SAMPLE 12 H P	Take 4 random samples, with replacement.
SAMPLE 12 H Q	" "
SAMPLE 12 H R	" "
SAMPLE 12 H S	" "
SUM P I	Sum the weight gains for the 4 resamples.
SUM Q J	" "
SUM R K	" "
SUM S L	" "
SUBTRACT I J IJ	Find the differences between all the possible pairs of resamples.

SUBTRACT I K IK   "   "

SUBTRACT I L IL   "   "

SUBTRACT J K JK   "   "

SUBTRACT J L JL   "   "

SUBTRACT K L KL   "   "

MULTIPLY IJ IJ IJSQ   Find the squared differences.

MULTIPLY IK IK IKSQ   "   "

MULTIPLY IL IL ILSQ   "   "

MULTIPLY JK JK JKSQ   "   "

MULTIPLY JL JL JLSQ   "   "

MULTIPLY KL KL KLSQ   "   "

ADD IJSQ IKSQ ILSQ JKSQ JLSQ KLSQ TOTAL
                  Add them together.

SCORE TOTAL Z   Keep track of the total for each trial.

END   End one trial, go back and repeat until 1000 trials are complete.

HISTOGRAM Z   Produce a histogram of the trial results.

COUNT Z >= 5299 K   Find out how many trials produced differences among groups as great as or greater than those observed.

DIVIDE K 1000 KK   Convert to a proportion.

Print the result.

We see that our observed sum of squares -- 5299 -- was exceeded by random draw sums of squares in only 3% of our trials. We conclude that the four treatments are likely not all similar.

NOTES:

[1]   Technical Note: The test described in this section is nonparametric and therefore makes no assumptions about the shapes of the distributions, which is good because we would be on soft ground if we assumed normality in the pig-ration case, given the sample sizes. This test does not, however, throw away information as do the rank and median tests illustrated earlier. And indeed, this test proves to be more powerful than the other nonparametric tests. After developing this test, I discovered that its general logic follows the tradition of the "randomization" tests, based on an idea by R.A. Fisher (1935, 1951) and worked out for the two-sample cases by E.J.G. Pitman (1937). But the only earlier mentions of sampling from the universe of possibilities are in M. Dwass (1957) and J.H. Chung and D. Fraser (1958). I am grateful to J. Pratt for bringing the latter literature to my attention.

[2]   The data are from The Liquor Handbook (1962, p. 68). Eight states are omitted for various reasons. For more information, see Simon and Simon (1987).

[3]   Various tests indicate that the difference between the groups of states is highly significant. See J.L. Simon (1966b).

[4]   Technical Note: Computing the sum of squared differences renders this test superficially more similar to the analysis of variance but will not alter the results. This test has not been discussed in the statistical literature, to my knowledge, except perhaps for a faint suggestion at the end of Chung and Fraser

(1958). This and the two-sample test can easily be performed with canned computer programs as well as RESAMPLING STATS. In addition to their advantages of nonparametricity, they are equally efficient and vastly easier to teach and to understand than the t-test and the analysis of variance. Therefore, I believe that these tests should be "treatments of choice," as the doctors say.

CHAPTER 9

CORRELATION AND CAUSATION

INTRODUCTION

EXAMPLE 9-1: Is Athletic Ability Directly Related to Intelligence?

EXAMPLE 9-2: Athletic Ability and I. Q. -- A Second Approach

EXAMPLE 9-3: Is There a Relationship Between Drinking Beer and Being In Favor of Selling Beer? (Testing For a Relationship Between Counted-Data Variables)

EXAMPLE 9-4: Do Athletes Really Have "Slumps"? (Are Successive Events in a Series Independent, or Is There a Relationship Between Them?)

PREVIEW

The correlation (speaking in a loose way for now) between two variables measures the strength of the relationship between them. A positive "linear" correlation between two variables x and y implies that high values of x are associated with high values of y, and that low values of x are associated with low values of y. A negative correlation implies the opposite; high values of x are associated with <u>low</u> values of y. By definition a "correlation coefficient" close to zero indicates little or no linear relationship between two variables; correlation coefficients close to 1 and -1 denote a strong positive or negative relationship. We will generally use a simpler measure of correlation than the correlation coefficient, however.

One way to measure correlation with the resampling method is to rank both variables from highest to lowest, and investigate how often in randomly-generated samples the rankings of the two variables are as close to each other as the rankings in the observed variables. A better approach, because it uses more of the quantitative information contained in the data though it requires more computation, is to multiply the values for the corresponding pairs of values for the two variables, and compare their sum to the analogous sum for randomly-generated pairs of the observed variable values. The last section of the chapter shows how the strength of a relationship can be determined when the data are counted, rather than being measured. First comes some discussion of the philosophical issues involved in correlation and causation.

INTRODUCTION TO CORRELATION AND CAUSATION

The questions in Examples 7-1 to 8-3 have been stated in the following form: Does the independent variable (say, irradiation; or type of pig ration) have an effect upon the dependent variable (say, sex of fruit flies; or weight gain of pigs)? This is another way to state this question: Is there a causal relationship between the independent variable(s) and the dependent variable? ("Independent" or "control" is the name we give to the variable(s) the researcher believes is (are) responsible for changes in the other variable, which we call the "dependent" or "response" variable).

A causal relationship cannot be defined perfectly neatly. Even an experiment does not determine perfectly whether a relationship deserves to be called "causal" because, among other reasons, the independent variable may not be clear-cut. For example, even if cigarette smoking experimentally produces cancer in rats, it might be the paper and not the tobacco that causes the cancer. Or consider the fabled gentlemen who got experimentally drunk on bourbon and soda on Monday night, scotch and soda on Tuesday night, and brandy and soda on Wednesday night -- and stayed sober Thursday night by drinking nothing. With a vast inductive leap of scientific imagination, they treated their experience as an empirical demonstration that soda, the common element each evening, was the cause of the inebriated state they had experienced. Notice that their deduction was perfectly sound, given only the recent evidence they had. Other knowledge of the world is necessary to set them straight. That is, even in a controlled experiment there is often no way except subject-matter knowledge to avoid erroneous conclusions about causality. Nothing except substantive knowledge or scientific intuition would have led them to the recognition that it is the alcohol rather than the soda that made them drunk, <u>as long as they always took soda with their drinks</u>. And no statistical procedure can suggest to them that they ought to experiment with the presence and absence of soda. If this is true for an experiment, it must also be true for an uncontrolled study.

Here are some tests that a relationship usually must pass to be called causal. That is, a working definition of a particular causal relationship is expressed in a statement that has these important characteristics:

(1) It is an association that is strong enough so that the observer believes it to have a predictive (explanatory) power great enough to be scientifically useful or interesting. For example, he is not likely to say that wearing glasses causes (or is a cause of) auto accidents if the observed correlation is .07, even if the sample is large enough to make the correlation statistically significant. In other words, unimportant relationships are not likely to be labeled causal.

Various observers may well differ in judging whether or not an association is strong enough to be important and therefore "causal". And the particular field in which the observer works may affect this judgment. This is an indication that whether or not a relationship is dubbed "causal" involves a good deal of human judgment and is subject to dispute.

(2) The "side conditions" must be sufficiently <u>few</u> and sufficiently observable so that the relationship will apply under a wide enough range of conditions to be considered useful or interesting. In other words, <u>the relationship must not require too many "if"s, "and"s, and "but"s in order to hold</u>. For example, one might say that an increase in income caused an increase in the birth rate if this relationship were observed everywhere. But, if the relationship were found to hold only in developed countries, among the educated classes, and among the higher-income groups, then it would be less likely to be called "causal" -- even if the correlation were extremely high once the specified conditions had been met. A similar example can be made of the relationship between income and happiness.

(3) For a relationship to be called "causal", there should be sound reason to believe that, even if the control variable were not the "real" cause (and it never is), other relevant "hidden" and "real" cause variables must also change consistently with changes in the control variables. That is, a variable being manipulated may reasonably be called "causal" if the real variable for which it is believed to be a proxy must always be tied intimately to it. (Between two variables, v and w, v may be said to be the "more real" cause and $\underline{w}$ a "spurious" cause, if $\underline{v}$ and $\underline{w}$ require the same side conditions, except that $\underline{v}$ does not require $\underline{w}$ as a side condition.) This third criterion (non-spuriousness) is of particular importance to policy makers. The difference between it and the previous criterion for side conditions is that a plenitude of very restrictive side conditions may take the relationship out of the class of causal relationships, even though the effects of the side conditions are known. This criterion of nonspuriousness concerns variables that are as yet unknown and unevaluated but that have a possible ability to upset the observed association.

Examples of spurious relationships and hidden-third-factor causation are commonplace. For a single example, toy sales rise in December. There is no danger in saying that December causes an increase in toy sales, even though it is "really" Christmas that causes the increase, because Christmas and December practically always accompany each other.

Belief that the relationship is not spurious is increased if many likely variables have been investigated and none removes the relationship. This is further demonstration that the test of whether or not an association should be called "causal" cannot be a logical one; there is no way that one can express in symbolic logic the fact that many other variables have been tried without changing the relationship in question.

(4) The more tightly a relationship is bound into (that is, deduced from, compatible with, and logically connected to) a general framework of theory, the stronger is its claim to be called "causal". For an economics example, observed positive relationships between the interest rate and business investment and between profits and investment are more likely to be called "causal" than is the relationship between

liquid assets and investment. This is so because the first two statements can be deduced from classical price theory, whereas the third statement cannot. Connection to a theoretical framework provides support for belief that the side conditions necessary for the statement to hold true are not restrictive and that the likelihood of spurious correlation is not great; because a statement is logically connected to the rest of the system, the statement tends to stand or fall as the rest of the system stands or falls. And, because the rest of the system of economic theory has, over a long period of time and in a wide variety of tests, been shown to have predictive power, a statement connected with it is cloaked in this mantle.

The social sciences other than economics do not have such well-developed bodies of deductive theory, and therefore this criterion of causality does not weigh as heavily in sociology, for instance, as in economics. Rather, the other social sciences seem to substitute a weaker and more general criterion, that is, whether or not the statement of the relationship is accompanied by other statements that seem to "explain" the "mechanism" by which the relationship operates. Consider, for example, the relationship between the phases of the moon and the suicide rate. The reason that sociologists do not call it causal is that there are no auxiliary propositions that explain the relationship and describe an operative mechanism. On the other hand, the relationship between broken homes and juvenile delinquency is often referred to as "causal" in large part, because a large body of psychoanalytic theory serves to explain why a child raised without one or the other parent, or in the presence of parental strife, should not adjust readily.

Furthermore, one can never decide with perfect certainty whether in any given situation one variable "causes" a particular change in another variable. At best, given your particular purposes in investigating a phenomena, you may be safe in judging that very likely there is causal influence.

In brief, it is correct to say (as it is so often said) that correlation does not prove causation -- if we add the word "completely" to make it "correlation does not completely prove causation". On the other hand, causation can never be "proven" completely by correlation or any other

206

tool or set of tools, including experimentation. The best we can do is make informed judgments about whether to call a relationship causal.

It is clear, however, that in any situation where we are interested in the possibility of causation, we must at least know whether there is a relationship (correlation) between the variables of interest; the existence of a relationship is necessary for a relationship to be judged causal even if it is not sufficient to receive the causal label. And in other situations where we are not even interested in causality, but rather simply want to predict events or understand the structure of a system, we may be interested in the existence of relationships quite apart from questions about causations. Therefore our next set of problems deals with the likelihood of there being a relationship between two measured variables, variables that can take on any values (say, the values on a test of athletic scores) rather than just two values (say, whether or not there has been irradiation.)

Another way to think about such problems is to ask whether two variables are independent of each other -- that is, whether you know anything about the value of one variable if you know the value of the other in a particular case -- or whether they are not independent but rather are related.

Example 9-1: Is Athletic Ability Directly Related to Intelligence? (Is There Correlation Between Two Variables or Are They Independent?) (Program "Ability1")

A scientist often wants to know whether or not two characteristics go together, that is, whether or not they are correlated (that is, related or associated). For example, do youths with high athletic ability tend to also have high I.Q.s?

Hypothetical physical-education scores of a group of ten high-school boys are shown in Table 9-1, ordered from high to low, along with the I.Q. score for each boy. The ranks for each student's athletic and I.Q. scores are then shown in columns 3 and 4.

Table 9-1			
HYPOTHETICAL ATHLETIC AND I.Q. SCORES FOR HIGH SCHOOL BOYS			
ATHLETIC SCORE (1)	I.Q. SCORE (2)	ATHLETIC RANK (3)	I.Q. RANK (4)
97	114	1	3
94	120	2	1
93	107	3	7
90	113	4	4
87	118	5	2
86	101	6	8
86	109	7	6
85	110	8	5
81	100	9	9
76	99	10	10

We want to know whether a high score on athletic ability tends to be found along with a high I.Q. score more often than would be expected by chance. Therefore, our strategy is to see how often high scores on both variables are found by chance. We do this by disassociating the two variables and making two separate and independent universes, one composed of the athletic scores and another of the I.Q. scores. Then we draw pairs of observations from the two universes at random, and compare the experimental patterns that occur by chance to what actually is observed to occur in the world.

The first testing scheme we shall use is similar to our first approach to the pig rations -- splitting the results into just "highs" and "lows." We take ten cards, one of each denomination from "ace" to "10", shuffle, and deal five cards to correspond to the first five athletic ranks. The face values then correspond to the I.Q. ranks. Under the benchmark hypothesis the athletic ranks will not be associated with the I.Q. ranks. Add the face values in the first five cards in each trial; the first hand includes 2, 4, 5, 6, and 9, so the sum is 26. Record, shuffle, and repeat perhaps ten times. Then compare the random results to the sum of the observed ranks of the five top athletes, which equals 17.

The following steps describe a slightly different procedure than that just described, because this one may be easier to understand:

Step 1. Convert the athletic and I.Q. scores to ranks. Then constitute a universe of spades, "ace" to "10," to correspond to the athletic ranks, and a universe of hearts, "ace" to "10," to correspond to the IQ ranks.

Step 2. Deal out the well-shuffled cards into pairs, each pair with an athletic score and an I.Q. score.

Step 3. Locate the cards with the top five athletic ranks, and add the I.Q. rank scores on their paired cards. Compare this sum to the observed sum of 17. If 17 or less, indicate "yes," otherwise "no." (Why do we use "17 or less" rather than "less than 17"? Because we are asking the probability of a score this low or lower.)

Step 4. Repeat steps 2 and 3 ten times.

Step 5. Calculate the proportion "yes." This estimates the probability sought.

In Table 9-2 we see that the observed sum is lower than the sum of the top 5 ranks in all but one (shown by an asterisk) of the ten random trials (trial 5), which suggests that there is a good chance (9 in 10) that the five best athletes will not have I.Q. scores that high by chance. But it might be well to deal some more to get a more reliable average. We add thirty hands, and thirty-nine of the total forty hands exceed the observed rank value, so the probability that the observed correlation of athletic and I.Q. scores would occur by chance is about .025. In other words, the odds are 39 to 1 against there being no association between athletic ability and I.Q. score, and it therefore seems reasonable to believe that high athletic ability tends to accompany a high I.Q.

Table 9-2

RESULTS OF 40 RANDOM TRIALS OF
THE PROBLEM "ABILITY"
(Note: Observed sum of IQ ranks: 17)

Trial	Sum of IQ Ranks	Yes or No
1	26	No
2	23	No
3	22	No
4	37	No
*5	16	Yes
6	22	No
7	22	No
8	28	No
9	38	No
10	22	No
11	35	No
12	36	No
13	31	No
14	29	No
15	32	No
16	25	No
17	25	No
18	29	No
19	25	No
20	22	No
21	30	No
22	31	No
23	35	No
24	25	No
25	33	No

Table 9-2 (Continued)		
Trial	Sum of IQ Ranks	Yes or No
26	30	No
27	24	No
28	29	No
29	30	No
30	31	No
31	30	No
32	21	No
33	25	No
34	19	No
35	29	No
36	23	No
37	23	No
38	34	No
39	23	No
40	26	No

The RESAMPLING STATS program "Ability1" creates an array containing the I.Q. rankings of the top 5 students in athletics. The SUM of these I.Q. rankings constitutes the observed result to be tested against randomly-drawn samples. We observe that the actual I.Q. rankings of the top five athletes sums to 17. The more frequently that the sum of 5 randomly-generated rankings (out of 10) is as low as this observed number, the higher is the probability that there is no relationship between athletic performance and I.Q. based on these data.

First we record the NUMBERS "1" through "10" into vector A. Then we SHUFFLE the numbers so that the rankings are in a random order. Then TAKE the first 5 of these numbers and put them in another array, D, and SUM them, putting the result in E. We repeat this procedure 1000 times, recording each result in a scorekeeping vector: Z. Graphing Z, we get a HISTOGRAM that shows us how often our randomly assigned sums exceed 17.

Program "ABILITY1"

REPEAT 1000	Repeat the experiment 1000 times.
NUMBERS 1,10 A	Constitute the set of I.Q. ranks.
SHUFFLE A B	Shuffle them.
TAKE B 1,5 D	Take the first 5 ranks.
SUM D E	Sum those ranks.
SCORE E Z	Keep track of the result of each trial.
END	End the experiment, go back and repeat.
HISTOGRAM Z	Produce a histogram of trial results.

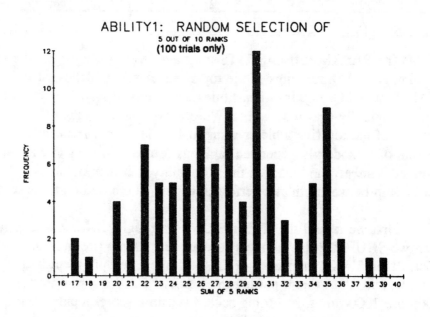

ABILITY1: RANDOM SELECTION OF
5 OUT OF 10 RANKS
(100 trials only)

We see that in only 2% of the trials did random selection of ranks produce a total of 17 or lower. RESAMPLING STATS will calculate this for us directly:

COUNT Z <= 17 K   Determine how many trials produced sums of ranks <= 17 by chance.

DIVIDE K 1000 KK   Convert to a proportion.

PRINT KK   Print the results.

Why do we sum the ranks of the first _five_ athletes and compare them with the second five athletes, rather than comparing the top three, say, with the bottom seven? Indeed, we could have looked at the top three, two, four, or even six or seven. The first reason for splitting the group in half is that an even split uses the available information more fully, and therefore we obtain greater efficiency. (I cannot prove this formally here, but perhaps it makes intuitive sense to you.) A second reason is that getting into the habit of always looking at an even split reduces the chances that you will pick and choose in such a manner as to fool yourself. For example, if the I.Q. ranks of the top five athletes were 3, 2, 1, 10, and 9, we would be deceiving ourselves if, after looking the data over, we drew the line between athletes 3 and 4. (More generally, choosing an appropriate measure before examining the data will help you avoid fooling yourself in such matters.)

A simpler but less efficient approach to this same problem is to classify the top-half athletes by whether or not they were also in the top half of the I.Q. scores. Of the first five athletes actually observed, _four_ were in the top five I.Q. scores. We can then shuffle five black and five red cards and see how often four or more (that is, four or five) blacks come up with the first five cards. The proportion of times that four or more blacks occurs in the trial is the probability that the observed scores come from the same universe, that is, that there is no association. Table 9-3 shows a proportion of five trials out of twenty, yielding a much weaker result than did the previous method.

Table 9-3
Results of 20 Random Trials of the Problem "ABILITY2"
Observed Score: 4

Trial	Score	Yes or No
1	4	Yes
2	2	No
3	2	No
4	2	No
5	3	No
6	2	No
7	4	Yes
8	3	No
9	3	No
10	4	Yes
11	3	No
12	1	No
13	3	No
14	3	No
15	4	Yes
16	3	No
17	2	No
18	2	No
19	2	No
20	4	Yes

In the RESAMPLING STATS program "Ability2" we first note that the top 5 athletes had 4 of the top 5 I.Q. scores. So we constitute the set of 10 IQ rankings (vector A). We then SHUFFLE A and TAKE 5 I.Q. rankings (out of 10). We COUNT how many are in the top 5, and keep SCORE of the result. After REPEATing 1000 times, we find out how often we select 4 of the top 5.

Program "ABILITY2"

REPEAT 1000	Do 1000 experiments.
NUMBERS 1,10 A	Constitute the set of I.Q. ranks.
SHUFFLE A B	Shuffle them.
TAKE B 1,5 C	Take the first 5 ranks.
COUNT C between 1 5 D	Of those 5, count how many are top half ranks (1-5).
SCORE D Z	Keep track of that result in Z
END	End one experiment, go back and repeat until all 1000 are complete.
COUNT Z >= 4 K	Determine how many trials produced 4 or more top ranks by chance.
DIVIDE K 1000 KK	Convert to a proportion.
PRINT KK	Print the result.

So far we have proceeded on the theory that if there is <u>any</u> relationship between athletics and I.Q., then the better athletes have higher rather than lower I.Q. scores. The justification for this assumption is that past research suggests that it is probably true. But if we had not had the benefit of that past research, we would then have had to proceed somewhat differently; we would have had to consider the possibility that the top five athletes could have I.Q. scores either higher or lower than those of the other students. The results of the "two-tail" test would have yielded odds weaker than those we observed.

Example 9-2: Athletic Ability and I.Q. a Second Way. (Program "Ability3").

Example 9-1 investigated the relationship between I.Q. and athletic score by ranking the two sets of scores. But ranking of scores loses some efficiency because it uses only an "ordinal" (rank-ordered) rather than a "cardinal" (measured) scale; the numerical shadings and relative relationships are lost when we convert to ranks. Therefore let us consider a test of correlation that uses the original cardinal numerical scores.

First a little background: Figures 9-1 and 9-2 show two hypothetical cases of very high association among the I.Q. and athletic scores used in previous examples. Figure 9-1 indicates that the higher the I.Q. score, the higher the athletic score. With a boy's athletic score you can thus predict quite well his I.Q. score by means of a hand-drawn line -- or vice versa. The same is true of Figure 9-2, but in the opposite direction. Notice that even though athletic score is on the x-axis (horizontal) and I.Q. score is on the y-axis (vertical), the athletic score does not cause the I.Q. score. (It is an unfortunate deficiency of such diagrams that some variable must arbitrarily be placed on the x axis, whether you intend to suggest causation or not.)

Hypothetical Data For a Group of Boys

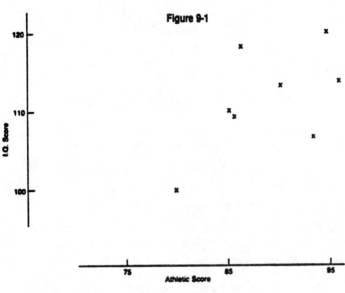

Figure 9-1

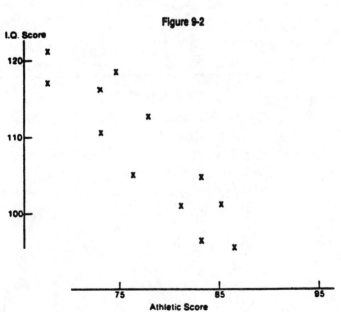

Figure 9-2

In Figure 9-3, which plots the scores as given in table 9-1 the prediction of athletic score given I.Q. score, or vice versa, is less clear-cut than in Figure 9-2. On the basis of Figure 9-3 alone, one can say only that there <u>might</u> be some association between the two variables.

Figure 9-3

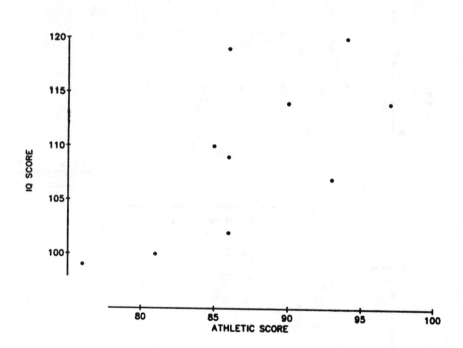

CORRELATION: SUM OF PRODUCTS

Now let us take advantage of a handy property of numbers. The more closely two sets of numbers match each other in order, the higher the sums of their products. Consider the following arrays of the numbers 1, 2, and 3:

$$1 \times 1 = 1$$
$$2 \times 2 = 4 \qquad \text{(columns in matching order)}$$
$$3 \times 3 = 9$$

$$\text{SUM} = 14$$

$$1 \times 2 = 2$$
$$2 \times 3 = 6 \qquad \text{(columns not in matching order)}$$
$$3 \times 1 = 3$$

$$\text{SUM} = 11$$

I will not attempt a mathematical proof, but the reader is encouraged to try additional combinations to be sure that the highest sum is obtained when the order of the two columns is the same.

Likewise, the lowest sum is obtained when the two columns are in perfectly opposite order:

$$1 \times 3 = 3$$
$$2 \times 2 = 4 \qquad \text{(columns in opposite order)}$$
$$3 \times 1 = 3$$

$$\text{SUM} = 10$$

Consider the cases in Table 9-4 which are chosen to illustrate a perfect (linear) association between x (Column 1) and $y1$ (Column 2), and also between x (Column 1) and $y2$ (Column 4); the numbers shown in Columns 3 and 5 are those that would be consistent with perfect associations. Notice the sum of the multiples of the x and y values in the two cases. It is either higher (xy1) or lower (xy2) than for any other possible way of arranging the y's. Any other arrangement of the y's ($y3$, in Column 6, for example, chosen at random), when multiplied by the x's in Column 1, ($xy3$), produces a sum that falls somewhere between the sums of $xy1$ and $xy2$, as is the case with any other set of $y3$'s which is not perfectly correlated with the x's.

Table 9-4						
Comparison of Sums of Multiplications						
	Strong Positive Relationship		Strong Negative Relationship		Random Pairings	
X	Y1	X*Y1	Y2	X*Y2	Y3	X*Y3
2	2	4	10	20	4	8
4	4	16	8	32	8	32
6	6	36	6	36	6	36
8	8	64	4	48	2	16
10	10	100	2	20	10	100
SUMS:		220		156		192

Table 9-5, below, shows that the sum of the products of the observed I.Q. scores multiplied by athletic scores (column 7) is **between** the sums that would occur if the I.Q. scores were ranked from best to worst (column 3) and worst to best (column 5). The extent of correlation (association) can thus be measured by whether the sum of the multiples of the observed x and y values is relatively much higher or much lower than are sums of randomly-chosen pairs of x and y.

Table 9-5
Sums of Products: IQ and Athletic Scores

3 Cases:

-- Perfect positive correlation (hypothetical); column 3
-- Perfect negative correlation (hypothetical); column 5
-- Observed; column 7

1	2	3	4	5	6	7
Athletic Score	Hypothetical I.Q.	Column 1 x Column 2	Hypothetical I.Q.	Column 1 x Column 4	Actual I.Q.	Column 1 x Column 6
97	120	11640	99	9603	114	11058
94	118	11092	100	9400	120	11280
93	114	10602	101	9393	107	9951
90	113	10170	107	9630	113	10170
87	110	9570	109	9483	118	10266
86	109	9374	110	8460	101	8686
86	107	9202	113	9718	109	9374
85	101	8585	114	9690	110	9350
81	100	8100	118	9558	100	8100
76	99	7524	120	9120	99	7524
		95859		95055		95759

Now we attack the I.Q. and athletic-score problem using the property of numbers just discussed. First multiply the x and y values of the actual observations, and sum them to be 95,759 (Table 9-5). Then write the ten observed I.Q. scores on cards, and assign the cards in random order to the ten athletes, as shown in column 1 in Table 9-6.

221

Table 9-6

Random Drawing of IQ Scores and Pairing Randomly Against Athletic Scores (20 Trials)

Athletic Score	Trial Number									
	1	2	3	4	5	6	7	8	9	10
97	114	109	110	118	107	114	107	120	100	114
94	101	113	113	101	118	100	110	109	120	107
93	107	118	100	99	120	101	114	99	110	113
90	113	101	118	114	101	113	100	118	99	99
87	120	100	101	100	110	107	113	114	101	118
86	100	110	120	107	113	110	118	101	118	101
86	110	107	99	109	100	120	120	113	114	120
85	99	99	104	120	99	109	101	107	109	109
81	118	120	114	110	114	99	99	100	107	109
76	109	114	109	113	109	118	109	110	113	110

Athletic Score	Trial Number									
	11	12	13	14	15	16	17	18	19	20
97	109	118	101	109	107	100	99	113	99	110
94	101	110	114	118	101	107	114	101	109	113
93	120	120	100	120	114	113	100	100	120	100
90	110	118	109	110	99	109	107	109	110	99
87	100	100	120	99	118	114	110	110	107	101
86	118	99	107	100	109	118	113	118	100	118
86	99	101	99	101	100	99	101	107	114	120
85	107	114	110	114	120	110	120	120	118	100
81	114	107	113	113	110	101	109	114	101	100
76	113	109	118	107	113	120	118	99	118	107

Multiply by the x's, and sum as in Table 9-7. If the I.Q. scores and athletic scores are <u>positively associated</u>, that is, if high I.Q.s and high athletic scores go together, then the sum of the multiplications for the observed sample will be higher than for most of the random trials. (If high I.Q.s go with low athletic scores, the sum of the multiplications for the observed sample will be <u>lower</u> than most of the random trials.)

Table 9-7

Results of Sum of Products for
Above 20 Random Trials

TRIAL	SUM OF MULTIPLICATIONS
1	95,430
2	95,426
3	95,446
4	95,381
5	95,542
6	95,362
7	95,508
8	95,590
9	95,379
10	95,532
11	95,406
12	95,622
13	95,250
14	95,599
15	95,323
16	95,308
17	95,220
18	95,443
19	95,421
20	95,528

More specifically, by the steps:

Step 1. Write the ten I.Q. scores on one set of cards, and the ten athletic scores on another set of cards.

Step 2. Pair the I.Q. and athletic-score cards at random. Multiply the scores in each pair, and add the results of the ten multiplications.

Step 3. Compare the experimental sum in step 2 to the observed sum, 95,759. If the experimental sum is as large or larger, record "yes", otherwise "no".

Step 4. Repeat steps 2 and 3 twenty times.

Step 5. Compute the proportion "yes", which estimates the probability that an association as strong as the observed would occur by chance.

The sums of the multiplications for 20 trials are shown in Table 9-7. No random-trial sum was as high as the observed sum, which suggests that the probability of an association this strong happening by chance is so low as to approach zero. (An empirically-observed probability is never actually zero).

This program can be solved particularly easily with RESAMPLING STATS. The arrays A and B in program "Ability3" list the athletic scores and the I.Q. scores respectively of 10 "actual" students ordered from highest to lowest athletic score. We MULTIPLY the corresponding elements of these arrays and proceed to compare the sum of these multiplications to the sums of experimental multiplications in which the elements are selected randomly.

Finally, we COUNT the trials in which the sum of the products of the randomly-paired athletic and I.Q. scores equals or exceeds the sum of the products in the observed data.

224

Program "ABILITY3"

NUMBERS (97 94 93 90 87 86 86 85 81 76) A
                         Record athletic scores, highest to lowest.

NUMBERS (114 120 107 113 118 101 109 110 100 99) B
                         Record corresponding IQ scores for those students.

MULTIPLY A B C   Multiply the two sets of scores together.

SUM C D   Sum the results.

REPEAT 1000   Do 1000 experiments.

   SHUFFLE A E   Shuffle the athletic scores so we can pair them against IQ scores.

   MULTIPLY E B F   Multiply the shuffled athletic scores by the I.Q. scores. (Note that we could shuffle the I.Q. scores too but it would not achieve any greater randomization.)

   SUM F J   Sum the randomized multiplications.

   SUBTRACT D J K   Subtract the sum from the sum of the "observed" multiplication.

   SCORE K Z   Keep track of the result in Z.

END   End one trial, go back and repeat until 1000 trials are complete.

HISTOGRAM Z   Obtain a histogram of the trial results.

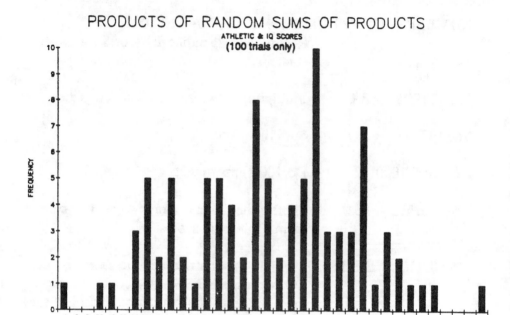

PRODUCTS OF RANDOM SUMS OF PRODUCTS
ATHLETIC & IQ SCORES
(100 trials only)

OBSERVED SUM LESS RANDOM SUM

We see that obtaining a chance trial result as great as that observed was rare. RESAMPLING STATS will calculate this proportion for us:

COUNT Z <= 0 K   Determine in how many trials the random sum of products was less than the observed sum of products.

DIVIDE K 1000 KK   Convert to a proportion.

PRINT KK

Example 9-3: Is There A Relationship Between Drinking Beer And Being In Favor of Selling Beer?   (Testing for a Relationship Between Counted-Data Variables.) (Program "Beerpoll")

The data for athletic ability and I.Q. were measured. Therefore, we could use them in their original "cardinal" form, or we would split them up into "high" and "low" groups. Often, however, the individual observations are recorded only as "yes" or "no", which makes it more difficult to ascertain the existence of a relationship. Consider the poll responses in Table 9-8 to two public-opinion survey questions: "Do you drink beer?" and "Are you in favor of local option on the sale of beer?" [2]

Table 9-8
Results of Observed Sample for Problem "Beerpoll"

Do you favor local option on the sale of beer?	Do you drink beer?		
	Yes	No	Total
Favor	37	20	57
Don't favor	15	6	21
Total	52	26	78

Here is the statistical question: Is a person's opinion on "local option" related to whether or not he drinks beer? Our resampling solution begins by noting that there are seventy-eight respondents, fifty-seven of whom approve local option and twenty-one of whom do not. Therefore write "approve" on fifty-seven index cards and "not approve" on twenty-one index cards. Now take another set of seventy-eight index cards, preferably of a different color, and write "yes" on fifty-two of them and "no" on twenty-six of them, corresponding to the numbers of

227

people who do and do not drink beer in the sample. Now lay them down in random <u>pairs</u>, one from each pile.

If there is a high association between the variables, then real life observations will bunch up in the two diagonal cells on either diagonal in Table 9-8. (Ignore the "total" data for now.) Therefore, subtract one sum of two diagonal cells from the other sum for the observed data: $(37 + 6) - (20 + 15) = 8$. Then compare this difference to the comparable differences found in random trials. The proportion of times that the simulated-trial difference does not exceed the observed difference is the probability that the observed association is not caused by chance. (Notice that, in this case, we are working on the assumption that beer drinking is <u>positively</u> associated with approval of local option and not the inverse. We are interested only in differences that are equal to or exceed +8 when the northeast-southwest diagonal is subtracted from the northwest-southeast diagonal.)

We can carry out a resampling test with this procedure:

Step 1. Write "approve" on 57 and "disapprove" on 21 red index cards, respectively; write "Drink" and "Don't drink" on 52 and 26 white cards, respectively.

Step 2. Pair the two sets of cards randomly, and count the numbers of the four possible pairs: "approve-drink," "disapprove-don't drink," "disapprove-drink," and "approve-don't drink." Record the number of these combinations, as in Table 9-9, where columns 1-4 correspond to the four cells in Table 9-8.

Table 9-9				
RESULTS OF 10 RANDOM TRIALS OF THE PROBLEM "BEERPOLL"				
Trial	(1) Approve Yes	(2) Approve No	(3) Disapprove Yes	(4) Disapprove No	(5) (Col 1 + Col 4) - (Col 2 + Col 3)
1	33	24	18	3	36-42=-6
2	38	19	14	7	45-33=12
3	39	18	13	8	47-31=16
4	38	19	14	7	45-33=12
5	35	22	17	4	39-39=0
6	35	22	16	5	40-38=2
7	38	19	14	7	45-33=12
8	40	19	12	9	49-31=18
9	42	17	12	9	51-29=22
10	37	20	15	6	43-35=8

Step 3. Add (column 1 plus column 4) and (column 2 plus column 3), and subtract the result in the second parenthesis from the result in the first parenthesis. If the difference is equal to or greater than 8, record "yes", otherwise "no".

Step 4. Repeat steps 2 and 3 perhaps a hundred times.

Step 5. Calculate the proportion "yes", which estimates the probability that an association this great or greater would be observed by chance.

A series of ten trials in this case (see Table 9-9) indicates that the observed difference is very often exceeded, which suggests that there is no relationship between beer drinking and opinion.

The RESAMPLING STATS program "Beerpoll" does the same work. From the "actual" sample results we know that 52 respondents drink beer and 26 do not. We create arrays A and B where A holds 52 "1"s for those who drink beer, and B holds 26 "2"s for those who do not. A CONCAT statement combines the respondents to this question into array C. The procedure for respondents to the question on the sale of beer is similar, 57 "1"s and 21 "2"s going into F. In the actual sample, 43 of the 78 respondents had "consistent" responses to the two questions -- that is, people who both favor the sale of beer <u>and</u> drink beer, or who are against the sale of beer <u>and</u> do not drink beer. We want to randomly pair the responses to the two questions to compare against that observed result to test the relationship.

To accomplish this aim, we REPEAT the following procedure 1000 times. We SHUFFLE C to G so that the responses are randomly ordered. Now when we SUBTRACT the corresponding elements of the two arrays, a "0" will appear in each element of the new array P for which there was consistency in the response of the two questions. We therefore COUNT the times that P equals "0" and place this result in I. Finally, we SCORE this value to Z for each trial, and then END the loop.

SCORE Z stores for each trial the number of pairs of responses which were consistent among the randomly-paired results. To determine whether the results of the actual sample indicate a relationship between the responses to the two questions, we check how often the random trials had as many "consistent" responses as the actual poll results. In the actual poll, 43 out of 78 respondents were "consistent" in their answers, so we COUNT the number of times that Z is greater than or equal to 43. This tells us the number of times out of 1000 that we would obtain randomly-paired responses as consistent as those provided by actual respondents.

Program "BEERPOLL"

SET 52 1 A	Constitute the set of 52 beer drinkers, represented by 52 1's.
SET 26 2 B	Constitute the set of 26 non-drinkers, represented by 2's.
CONCAT A B C	Bring them together in C.
SET 57 1 D	Constitute the set of 57 who favor allowing the sale of beer.
SET 21 2 E	Constitute the set of 21 who are against the sale of beer.
CONCAT D E F	Bring the latter two sets together in F.
Note:	F is now the vector {1 1 1 1 1 1 ... 2 2 2 2 2 ...} where 1 = people in favor, 2 = people opposed.
REPEAT 1000	Repeat the experiment 1000 times.
SHUFFLE C G	Shuffle the beer drinkers together with the non-drinkers, call the shuffled set G.
Note:	G is now a vector like {1 1 1 2 1 2 2 1 2 1 1 2 2 ...} where 1 = drinker, 2 = non-drinker.
SUBTRACT G F H	Subtract the favor/don't favor set from the drink/don't drink set. Consistent responses are someone who drinks favoring the sale of beer (a 1 and a 1) or someone who doesn't drink opposing the sale of beer. When subtracted, consistent responses produce a 0.

COUNT H =0 J	Count the number of consistent responses.
SCORE J Z	Keep track of the results of each trial.
END	End one trial, go back and repeat until all 1000 trials are complete.
HISTOGRAM Z	Produce a histogram of the trial result.

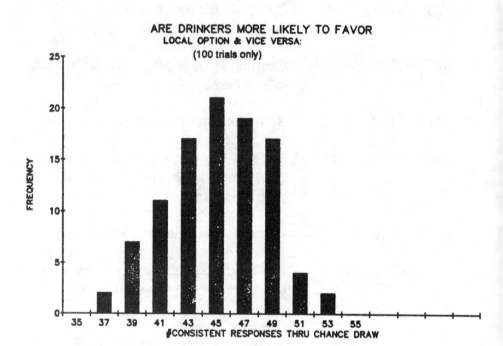

The actual results showed 43 "consistent" results. In the histogram we see that 80% of the trials produced 43 or more "consistent" results just by chance pairing -- without any relationship between the two variables. Hence, we conclude that there is little evidence of a relationship between the two variables.

Though the test just described may <u>generally</u> be appropriate for data of this sort, it may well not be appropriate in some particular case. Let's consider a set of data where even if the test showed that an association existed, we would not believe the test result to be meaningful.

Suppose the survey results had been as presented in Table 9-10. We see that non-beer drinkers have a higher rate of approval of allowing beer drinking, which does not accord with experience or reason. Hence, without additional explanation we would not believe that a meaningful relationship exists among these variables even if the test showed one to exist. (Still another reason to doubt that a relationship exists is that the absolute differences are too small -- there is only a 6% difference in disapproval between drink and don't drink groups -- to mean anything to anyone. On both grounds, then, it makes sense simply to act as if there were no difference between the two groups and to run <u>no test</u>.)

Table 9-10
Beer Poll in Which Results are not
in Accord with Expectation or Reason

	% Approve	% Disapprove	Total
Beer Drinkers	71%	29%	100%
Non-Beer Drinkers	77%	23%	100%

The lesson to be learned from this is that one should inspect the data carefully before applying a statistical test, and only test for "significance" if the apparent relationships accord with theory, general understanding, and common sense.

The important concept of independent events was introduced earlier, in Chapter 3. Various scientific and statistical decisions depend upon whether or not a series of events is independent. But how does one know whether or not the events are independent? Let us consider a baseball example.

Baseball players and their coaches believe that on some days and during some weeks a player will bat better than on other days and during other weeks. And team managers and coaches act on the belief that there are periods in which players do poorly -- slumps -- by temporarily replacing the player with another after a period of poor performance. The underlying belief is that a series of failures indicates a temporary (or permanent) change in the player's capacity to play well, and it therefore makes sense to replace him until the evil spirit passes on, either of its own accord or by some change in the player's style.

But even if his hits come randomly, a player will have runs of good luck and runs of bad luck just by chance -- just as does a card player. The problem, then, is to determine whether (a) the runs of good and bad batting are merely runs of chance, and the probability of success for each event remains the same throughout the series of events -- which would imply that the batter's ability is the same at all times, and coaches should not take recent performance heavily into account when deciding which players should play; or (b) whether a batter really does have a tendency to do better at some times than at others, which would imply that there is some relationship between the occurrence of success in one trial event and the probability of success in the next trial event, and therefore that it is reasonable to replace players from time to time.

Let's analyze the batting of a player we shall call "Slug". Here are the results of Slug's first 100 times at bat during the 1987 season ("H" = hit, "X" = out):

X X X X X X H X X H X H H X X X X X X X X X H X X X
X X H X X X X H H X X X X X H X X H X H X X X H H X X X
X X H X H X X X X H H X H H X X X X X X X X X X X H X X X
H X X H X X H X H X X H X X X H X X X.

Now, do Slug's hits tend to come in bunches? That would be the case if he really did have a tendency to do better at some times than at others. Therefore, let us compare Slug's results with those of a deck of cards or a set of random numbers that we know has no tendency to do better at some times than at others.

During this period of 100 times at bat, Slug has averaged one hit in every four times at bat -- a .250 batting average. This average is the same as the chance of one card suit's coming up. We designate hearts as "hits" and prepare a deck of 100 cards, twenty-five "H"s (hearts, or "hit") and seventy-five "X"s (other suit, or "out"). Here is the sequence in which the 100 randomly-shuffled cards fell:

X X H X X X X X H H X X X H H H X X X X X H X X X H
X X H X X X X H X H H X X X X X X X X X X H X X X X X H
H X X X X X H H H X X X X X X H X H X H X X H X H X H X X X
X X X X X H X X X X X X X H H H X X.

Now we can compare whether or not Slug's hits are bunched up more than they would be by random chance; we can do so by <u>counting the clusters</u> (also called "runs") of consecutive hits and outs for Slug and for the cards. Slug had forty-three clusters, which is more than the thirty-seven clusters in the cards; it therefore does not seem that there is a tendency for Slug's hits to cluster together. (A larger number of clusters indicates a lower tendency to cluster.)

Of course, the single trial of 100 cards shown above might have an unusually high or low number of clusters. To be safer, lay out, (say,) ten trials of 100 cards each, and compare Slug's number of clusters with the various trials. The proportion of trials with more clusters than Slug's indicates whether or not Slug's hits have a tendency to bunch up. (But caution: This proportion cannot be interpreted directly as a probability.)

Now the steps:

Step 1. Let "01-25" = hits, "26-00" = outs (X), Slug's long-run average.

Step 2. Write a series of "H's" or "X's" corresponding to 100 numbers, each selected randomly between 1 and 100.

Step 3. Count the number of "clusters", that is, the number of "runs" of the same event, "H's" or" X's".

Step 4. Compare the outcome in step 3 with Slug's outcome, 37 clusters. If 36 or fewer or more; write "yes", otherwise "no."

Step 5. Repeat steps 2-4 a hundred times.

Step 6. Compute the proportion "yes". This estimates the probability that Slug's record is not characterized by more "slumps" than would be caused by chance.

In RESAMPLING STATS, we can do this experiment 1000 times.

Program "SLUGGO"

REPEAT 1000

SET 3 0 A	Let 0 = out; A is a vector of three 0's
SET 1 1 B	Let 1 = hit; B is a vector of one 1
CONCAT A B C	Combine A and B in a single vector C
SAMPLE 100 C D	Sample 100 "at-bats" from C
RUNS D >=1 E	How many runs (of any length >=1) are there in the 100 at-bats?

SCORE E Z

END

HISTOGRAM Z

Examining the histogram, we see that 43 runs is not at all an unusual occurrence:

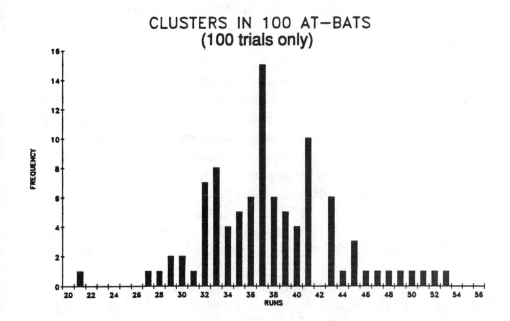

CLUSTERS IN 100 AT-BATS
(100 trials only)

The manager wants to look at this matter in a somewhat different fashion, however. He insists that the existence of slumps is proven by the fact that the player sometimes does not get a hit for an abnormally long period of time. One way of testing whether or not the coach is right is by comparing an average player's longest slump in a 100-at-bat season with the longest run of outs in the first card trial. Assume that Slug is a player picked at random. Then compare Slug's longest slump, -- say, 10 outs in a row -- with the longest cluster of a single simulated 100-at-bat trial with the cards, 9 outs. This result suggests that Slug's apparent slump might well have resulted by chance.

The estimate can be made more accurate by taking the average longest slump (cluster of outs) in ten simulated 400-at-bat trials. But notice that we do not compare Slug's slump against the longest slump found in ten such simulated trials. We want to know the longest cluster of outs that would be found under average conditions, and the hand with the <u>longest</u> slump is <u>not</u> average or typical. Determining whether to compare Slug's slump with the <u>average</u> longest slump or with the <u>longest</u> of the ten longest slumps is a decision of crucial importance. There are no mathematical or logical rules to help you. What is required is hard, clear thinking. Experience can help you think clearly, of course, but these decisions are not easy or obvious even to the most experienced statisticians.

The coach may then refer to the protracted slump of one of the twenty-five players on his team to prove that slumps really occur. But, of twenty-five random 100-at-bat trials, one will contain a slump longer than any of the other twenty-four, and that slump will be considerably longer than average. A fair comparison, then, would be between the longest slump of his longest-slumping player, and the longest run of outs found among twenty-five random trials. In fact, the longest run among twenty-five hands of 100 cards was fifteen outs in a row. And, if we had set some of the hands for lower (and higher) batting averages than .250, the longest slump in the cards would have been even longer.

Research by Roberts and his students at the University of Chicago shows that in fact slumps do <u>not</u> exist, as I conjectured in the first publication of this material in 1969. (Of course, a batter feels as if he has a better chance of getting a hit at some times than at other times. After a series of successful at-bats, sandlot players and professionals alike feel confident -- just as gamblers often feel that they're on a "streak". But there seems to be no connection between a player's performance and whether he feels hot or cold, astonishing as that may be.)

Averages over longer periods may vary systematically, as Ty Cobb's annual batting average varied non-randomly from season to season, Roberts found. But short-run analyses of day-to-day and week-to-week individual and team performances in most sports have shown results similar to the outcomes that a lottery-type random-number machine would produce.

Gilovich, Vallone, and Twersky recently performed a similar study of basketball. First they determined that 91 percent of the fans at their universities believe that a player has "a better chance of making a shot after having just made his last two or three shots than he does after having just missed his last two or three shots." Then they examined the records of shots from the floor by the Philadelphia '76ers, foul shots by the Boston Celtics, and a shooting experiment using Cornell University teams. They found that though "players and fans alike tend to believe that a player's chance of hitting a shot are greater following a hit than following a miss on the previous shot," their analyses "provided no evidence for a positive correlation between the outcomes of successive shots." That is, knowing whether a shooter has or has not scored on the previous shot -- or in any previous sequence of shots -- is useless for predicting whether he will score again.

The species homo sapiens apparently has a powerful propensity to believe that one can find a pattern even when there is no pattern to be found. Two decades ago I cooked up several series of random numbers that looked like weekly prices of publicly-traded stocks. Players in the experiment were told to buy and sell stocks as they chose. Then I repeatedly gave them "another week's prices," and allowed them to buy and sell again. The players did all kinds of fancy calculating, using a wild variety of assumptions -- although there was no possible way that the figuring could help them.

When I stopped the game before completing the 10 buy-and-sell sessions they expected, subjects would ask that the game go on. Then I would tell them that there was no basis to believe that there were patterns in the data, because the "prices" were just randomly-generated numbers. Winning or losing therefore did not depend upon the subjects' skill. Nevertheless, they demanded that the game not stop until the 10 "weeks" had been played, so they could find out whether they "won" or "lost."

This study of batting illustrates how one can test for independence among various trials. The trials are independent if each observation is randomly chosen with replacement from the universe, in which case there is no reason to believe that one observation will be related to the observations directly before and after; as it is said, "the coin has no memory".

The year-to-year level of Lake Michigan is an example in which observations are <u>not</u> independent. If Lake Michigan is very high in one year, it is likely to be higher than average the following year because some of the high level carries over from one year into the next. [3] We could test this hypothesis by writing down whether the level in each year from, say, 1860 to 1975 was higher or lower than the median level for those years. We would then count the number of runs of "higher" and "lower" and compare the number of runs of "black" and "red" with a deck of that many cards; we would find fewer runs in the lake level than in an average hand of 116 (1976-1860) cards, though this test is hardly necessary. (But are the <u>changes</u> in Lake Michigan's level independent from year to year? If the level went up last year, is there a better than 50-50 chance that the level will also go up this year? The answer to this question is not so obvious. One could compare the numbers of runs of ups and downs against an average hand of cards, just as with the hits and outs in baseball.)

Exercise for students: How could one check whether the successive numbers in a random-number table are independent?

NOTES:

[1]   For a much fuller discussion see Simon and Burstein, (1985, Chapter 35), or previous editions by Simon (1960; 1979).

[2]   These data are from an example in W. J. Dixon and F. J. Massey (1957, p. 226), in which the problem is tackled conventionally with a chi-square test.

[3]   Example from W. A. Wallis (1957).

APPENDIX 1: A LESSON IN RESAMPLING STATISTICS
Julian L. Simon

Teacher ("T"): Good morning. Let's talk about poker. What is the chance of getting a pair of two cards of the same denomination -- two fives, say, or two queens -- in a hand of five cards dealt to you?

Student Abel: 1 in 5.

T: What do you mean by "1 in 5"?

Students: [Silence]

T: You mean that every single time you deal five hands you can expect to get a pair?

Doug: One in five times on the average.

T: How <u>sure</u> are you that it's one in five?

Abel: Well, it seems to me that I usually get a pair about every five times.

T: What would you say if I told you it's not one in five, but instead the chances are 1 in 2?

Becky: I'd say "Prove it".

T: Who said "Prove it?"

Becky: Me -- I say it's about one in twenty.

T: So we've got a variety of views here -- one in twenty, one in five, one in two. How would you go about finding out who's right?

Becky: Ask an expert.

T: Well, that's one possibility. Getting advice from people who know a lot about a subject is always a wise first tactic. But how would you know for sure whether the so-called expert knows what she or he is talking about? Finding an expert who is really an expert is not easy unless you are an expert yourself.

Let's assume that you don't have a tested expert handy. How would you go about finding a reliable answer on your own?

Charlie: Calculate from how many cards are in the deck, and how many cards you have. Use a formula.

T: Okay, how exactly should we calculate? Does anyone here know what the right formula is?

[Silence]

T: Does that mean that we are stuck? Is there anything we can do if we don't know the formula? And by the way, people often think they know the right formula but don't, and therefore calculate the wrong answer. That is a very big danger unless you are a skilled mathematician. Is there anything we can do now?

Charlie: Deal some hands.

T: Deal some hands? That's a wild and radical idea. [Laughter] What do you mean?

Charlie: Deal some cards.

T: Give us an example of what you mean.

Charlie: Play poker and keep track.

T: Let's be more specific. How would you do it?

Charlie: Okay, deal five cards --

T: Well, just by coincidence I brought a few cards with me.

[Dumps thirty decks of cards on the table.] Pass them around. Charlie, tell us exactly what to do with the cards. You're the boss. Stand up here in front and give us instructions.

[Charlie gets up and comes up front]

Charlie: Okay, you students [laughter] this is what we're going to do. Everybody deal out five cards.

Becky: Do we shuffle the deck first?

T: Good question. Should they shuffle, Charlie?

Charlie: First shuffle the deck and then deal five cards.

[Students shuffle and deal a hand.]

Charlie: How many of you have a pair?

[Students raise their hands if they have a pair.]

T: [Charlie] Now what?

Charlie: We can say that the chances are 7 out of 12 [the number who have a pair among the 12 students] that you get a pair.

T: [To the class] Does that do it? Is that our answer?

Abel: Next time we might get a different number of pairs.

T: Why is that?

Abel: Because the results differ from deal to deal.

T: Very important. Very, very important. The difference from trial to trial is one of the key ideas in probability and statistics -- is the idea of random variability. The results vary from one event to the next. A large proportion of the world's mistakes in business, sports, and politics occur because people do not recognize random variability for what is, and instead attach some meaning to the pattern in one particular trial. So what should we do about the random variability?

Becky: Deal the cards again and again, and mark down the results.

T: So we must keep track of the results. Alright, Becky, you're in charge now, tell us what to do.

Becky: Everybody shuffle your cards.

Doug: Do we have to shuffle the cards? How about just dealing a second hand from the deck? Would it make a difference whether we do that, or instead shuffle the deck and deal out five cards from the entire shuffled deck?

[Becky is silent.]

T: What do you all think? Does it make a difference whether we simply deal a second hand from the unshuffled deck, or shuffle and start again?

[Some hubbub, various voices and opinions]

T: So there is a difference of opinion. How should we settle the difference of opinion?

[Silence]

T: We can't answer every question at once. Let's assume for the moment that it doesn't matter, but let's also agree that we will settle the question later by the best possible method -- that is, try it out both ways. May I have your permission to postpone?

Of course if we do replace the five cards in the hand we deal, and use the entire deck, Doug's comment is very important, because if you replace the cards and <u>don't shuffle them</u> you have a big problem.

Now what, Becky?

Becky: Deal another hand.

Charlie: Wait a minute. How many people are playing in this game? You could have like five people playing, or three people playing. Wouldn't that make a difference?

T: You say the chances might be different if you had five people playing or three people. That's a very interesting question. But let's put that aside for the moment, and go on with what we were doing.

Essie: Shuffle them up and do it again.

T: How many times are we going to do this, Essie?

Essie: Everyone should deal ten hands.

T: You're the boss, Becky, tell people what to do.

Becky: Everybody, ten times, deal a hand, see if you have a pair, write down what you get. Do the whole thing ten times.

[Much dealing and writing]

Becky: Each of you tell me how many pairs you got.

[Gets the results and writes them on the board.]

T: So what's the answer, Becky?

Becky: The chances are 55 out of 120.

T: What's that as a fraction, and as a probability?

Abel: Eleven twenty-fourths, or about 46 per cent.

T: Are 120 hands enough?   Foxey: Yeah.

T: Well, 120 hands <u>might</u> be enough. Obviously it depends on how accurate you want to be, right? If we had more time, we could deal out another 120 hands, and compare the result. If there wasn't much difference we could be satisfied. Or we could do it again and again. And sooner or later we would get enough accuracy to safely play poker with, which is what we are interested in here.

So that's how you could go about finding out the chances of getting one pair or two pair or a royal flush in poker. If you tried to figure it out mathematically it might take you a lot longer to learn what you need to know. You might have to wait a few years until you go to college and then take two courses or six courses in probability theory, then work out the formula, and even then there would still be a fair chance you would wind up with the wrong formula. But with the method you all have just worked out, you're going to get a very good answer.

Now, What are the chances of getting a seven in two throws of the dice? Of course you've all lived very sheltered lives and none of you have ever seen a pair of dice before, right? [laughter] So what are the chances of throwing a seven?

[Silence]

Doug: Throw the dice and see.

T: Good move, Doug. Throw the dice once, and then what?

Doug: Write down what happens.

T: Then what?

Doug: Do it again.

T: Alright, Doug, you're the boss. You get it done.

Narrator: Doug runs the class experiment, which we won't show to save time.

T: Now let's consider a different kind of problem. Let's say that somebody comes along and says, what are the chances if I have four children that three of those children will be girls? How would you go about finding that out?

Foxey: Shuffle up a bunch of kids and deal out four.

[Laughter]

T: Sounds fine in theory, but it might be a bit difficult to actually carry out...How about some other suggestions?.

Essie: Have four kids and see what you get.

T: Sounds good. But let's say you have four children once. Is that going to be enough to give you a decent answer?

Charley: No. You need more families.

T: How many families do we need?

Charley: How about a hundred families?

T: So you're going to produce a hundred families. That's reasonable. But it could take you a little while to have a hundred families, a little strength and energy and money. So we scratch our heads and say, hold on here. Producing a hundred families is a very sensible idea, but it doesn't seem to be practical at the moment. Another suggestion?

Doug: Take a survey.

T: What do you mean by "take a survey"?

Doug: You go around and ask people who have four children how many are girls.

T: Super idea. Absolutely super. A survey is a terrific idea because it focuses us on trying to get an answer to a problem like this one by going out and looking at the world instead of just trying to do mathematics. Nothing wrong with mathematics, but there's always a great deal to be said for trying to get the answer by going out into the world and looking. How many families are you going to survey, Doug?

Doug: A hundred.

T: Any particular families?

Doug: Families with four children.

T: What are you going to ask the hundred families?

Doug: How many of your children are girls?

T: You're going to find a hundred families that have four kids, and ask each one how many are girls. Sounds good. Any problems?

Essie: It's going to take a lot of time to find a hundred families with four kids.

T: Yes, but it's a lot quicker than growing a hundred families. I'll bet if the twelve of you went out now, by the end of the day you could find a hundred families with four children and you could get a pretty good answer to this.

T: Let's try it. Okay teacher?

Regular class teacher: We have some other things we have to do today, unfortunately.

T: Okay, but let's remember that we could try it, and as scientists that would be an excellent way to do it.

T: Is there another way we can tackle the problem? What else can we do? Let's say that some businessperson comes in here and says, "I'm going to give you a thousand dollars if you can come up with a pretty good answer inside of one hour." You don't have time to take a survey. What would you do?

Think about it for a few minutes. Keep in mind that a good solution might be worth a thousand bucks. That should be enough to make you think.

Foxey: You can think about your friends's families that have four kids, and count how many of them have three girls.

T: Terrific idea. That's like taking a survey, but a lot faster. Maybe that will get you the thousand dollars.

Without in any way being critical of that terrific idea, let's ask how else might you go about it. Think back to the first problems we solved with poker and dice.

Charlie: Simulation.

T: Simulation? What's a simulation?

Charlie: You take something like a four-sided die or something like that.

T: In other words, you want to do something here in the classroom which is like having kids. Can somebody get more specific?

Essie: We could put an equal number of red and black balls in a pot, and pull four of them out. That would be like a family.

T: Does that make sense?

Several students: Yeah.

T: Essie, how many balls are you going to put in the pot?

Essie: Four of each.

T: How about if we put in two of each -- two red and two black -- and you reach in and you mush them around and take out four.

Essie: That wouldn't work.

T: Why not?

Essie: Because you'd have to have at least three red ones.

T: Exactly. So you couldn't possibly get three red ones if you only had four balls, two red and two black. How about if you only had six balls in there?

Essie: That wouldn't work, either.

T: Why wouldn't it work?

Essie: Because you couldn't have a combination of all girls.

T: That's right. If every combination isn't possible, there obviously is something wrong. Now what about four red and four black?

George: The chance of getting four girls would still be pretty small.

T: Let's see what is going on when we only have a few balls in the pot? What is the chance of having a girl the first time you have a child?

Class voices: Fifty-fifty. One in two. Fifty percent. etc.

T: If you have four red and four black balls, what is the chance of getting one red one? Becky?

Becky: Fifty per cent.

T: What is the chance of having a girl the second time a real family has a child?

Becky: Fifty per cent again, I guess.

T: Now, what is the chance of drawing a red ball from a pot that starts with four red and four black, after you draw a red ball?

Doug: Three in seven, which is less than fifty percent.

T: Right you are, Doug. So you can see why we can't have a pot with just three red or three black, or 4 and 4, or 10 and 10, for the same sort of reason.

Foxey: But if we have a big pot of both red and black balls, it would almost be okay, wouldn't it?

T: You're right, Foxey. That would be a very satisfactory approximation. But we would need a lot of balls.

Is there some other method we could use to get around this problem?

Let's try someone we haven't heard from lately. George, what would you do? How would you go about it? What are you going to put into the pot and how are you going to deal with it?

George: How about putting just two balls in, one red and one black, and put the ball back after you draw it?

T: Bingo. You've got it exactly. We call this "sampling with replacement", meaning that we put the ball back each time to keep the chance of drawing a red one the same.

George, tell us exactly how we would go about making an estimate of the chances of getting three girls in four children using just the two balls.

George: Draw a ball, and write down what color it is. Repeat that four times. Count the number of red balls. If the number is "3", write down "yes", otherwise write down "no".

T: Is once through enough?

George: Do the whole operation about a hundred times.

T: Does that make sense, class?

251

Class voices: Yeah, yes, okay...

T: That procedure would work quite well. But we don't have any balls. Essie, you suggested the balls. Is there any way that we could use this thing instead? [Holds up a quarter.]

Essie: I suppose we could flip a coin and the head could be like red, like a girl, and the tail like black.

T: Absolutely. And a coin will be easier to think about later on. So -- how would we do it with a coin?

George: Flip the coin, Teach.

T: [Flips]. Heads. Now what?

George: Record it.

T: You do it, George. Now what are we going to do next?

George: Do it four times.

T: Ok, do it George.

[Does it]

T: What happened?

George: Two and two.

T: What does that mean?

George: It means we didn't get three girls.

T: Now what?

George: We've got to do it a lot of times.

T: Can you get the class to help you, George? Yes? Then go

ahead and do it. Come on up here and do it. I suggest you put the results on the blackboard.

George [comes up to front]: Everybody take a coin, flip it, write down what you get, and do that four times.

[All do it]

George: What did you get? Abel? [Writes on board] Becky? [Etc.]

T: What do the results say, George?

George: The results say that 2 out of 12 times we get three girls.

Charlie: What happens if we get four girls? Do we count that?

Narrator: Here there is discussion about whether four girls should be counted. T ends by emphasizing that the decision should be made with an eye to the purpose for which the estimate is being developed.

T: Let's continue. Do we have enough trials?

Essie: With only 12, we might get different results next time.

T: Okay, how many more trials should we do?

Essie: Let's do a hundred altogether.

T: Okay, let's let George do it. [A couple of students groan at the joke.]

Narrator: George presides over a hundred trials and compiles the results from each student on the blackboard.

T: What do we do with the results, Essie?

Essie: We count the number of yes's and make a ratio.

T: A ratio of what?

Essie: The ratio of yes's to yes's plus no's, because we want to know what proportion of all the times we get yes, right? So we compute the ratio of the yes's to all the times we tried, all the families we had. And that will be our answer.

T: Sounds good to me. When the guy with the thousand bucks comes storming in here and says, "Have you got my answer?," we can say, "Ah yes," very coolly. And we'll be a thousand dollars richer.

Foxey: I have a question. Do an equal number of boys and girls get born? Are boys fifty per cent?

T: That is an important question. And the answer is "No." About 105 boys are born for every 100 girls, or 106 or 104, depending on the country. Now I ask you, Foxey, is the fact that the ratio is, say, 105 to 100, rather than 100 to 100, a difference big enough to spoil our method here?

Foxey: No.

T: Why not?

Foxey: Because 100 to 100 might be close enough.

T: Yes, you are right that we're interested in getting an answer which we can consider close enough for what we want to do. In practical life we're never interested in getting a perfectly accurate answer, because there is never a perfectly accurate answer. That is, the question is only whether 100 to 100 rather than 105 to 100 is good enough for our purposes here. But that means we've got to ask what our purposes are here.

Maybe we should ask the person who's offering to give you a thousand dollars, "What do you want this estimate for?" And if this person says, "Well I want to go into business making boys clothes and girls clothes," then probably an answer which is off by as much as would be caused by 100-100 instead of 105-100 wouldn't cause much harm. If we were trying to aim a rocket at the moon, however, this procedure might cause us to be off target by thousands of miles. In that case we would be sensible to pay more attention to the accuracy and carry out the procedure a bit differently. So it is crucial always to know just how much accuracy we need.

Let's say that the 105 to 100 isn't all that much of a problem for our purposes, and assume it's fifty-fifty for convenience.

We're doing terrifically. The only problem is that this cardshuffling and coinflipping takes time, and in more complex problems it would take even more time. So let's speed up the work with a handy-dandy card-dealer and coin-flipper called a computer, this machine here. We're going to make this machine do the same thing that we did with our coins. But we've got to tell this machine some special words to get it to do what we want it to do, because it is not as smart as you kids are.

Let's get the computer to flip coins for us, or rather, to do something which "simulates" flipping coins, which in turn simulates having children. Of course the machine doesn't really flip coins. Rather, it only deals with symbols like numbers and letters. So let's let "1" be a girl, and "2" be a boy.

Before we begin to write a program, we've got to do the really hard stuff, like figuring out how to turn the machine on.

Narrator: Here we briefly show how to insert a floppy disk, find the "On" switch, and call up the program RESAMPLING STATS with the command "Stats". The students also are shown how to begin with the main menu [show] and get a file [show] and then edit a file [show cursor movement] and afterwards how to run the file from the main menu. They are also shown that there is a tutorial for them to study when they are alone.

T: We first give the computer a command that tells it to make numbers. The command we use to make numbers is "generate."

You must spell each of these commands exactly, and provide it exactly the information it requires. If you write "yenerate" or "venerate" the machine isn't going to understand you, although if we wanted to, we could write a program that would correctly read most of our errors. But ordinarily the computer is very, very specific. You've got to get it right. But if you get the commands right, the computer won't make a mistake. So it's a pretty good deal -- you do your part correctly, and the machine will do its part correctly.

We want to generate four numbers, "1"s and "2"s, chosen randomly just like flipping a coin. So we look in the Manual, or on this "Quick List," which tells us that the first number we write after "generate" specifies to the computer how many numbers to generate randomly, using a random-number device inside the computer that works like a lottery.

How many numbers do we need?

Doug: A hundred.

T: That might be the number of families we want to create. But first we must tell the computer how many children in one family, just as in our first step when working with coins we decided how many times to flip a coin to get one family in our first step.

Foxey: Four numbers.

T: Okay, we write "GENERATE (4)"

The Manual tells us that the next part of the GENERATE command is the numbers the computer is going to make for us. Let's make it one's and two's, but it could be "zero's" and "one's" or whatever. So we're going to randomly generate four numbers that are either "1" or "2".

Now we must put these numbers someplace so that we can keep track of them. We tell the computer to put them in a little slot someplace, and we'll call that slot "A", a special location in the computer. So we write "GENERATE (4) (1,2) (A)".   Up until now I have been putting parentheses around what we call the "parameters" of the command. The Apple program requires that we do that. But for the IBM program the parentheses are not necessary, and a space between the parameters is sufficient to do what we call "delimit" each parameter. From here on I'll leave off the parentheses for convenience.

Now we must tell the computer to count how many girls are born. The next command logically is called "count". The Manual says that we must first tell the computer <u>where</u> to count. So we tell the computer to look in location A where we had put the result from the previous step.

Next we tell the computer <u>what</u> to count in A -- the number of "1"s for girls -- and where to put the <u>result</u> of the COUNT, which we decide will be location J. The command then is COUNT A = 1 J.

These actions by the computer simulate what we do with coins. We have now constructed one family with those two commands.

We must keep a record of this result, so we put it on a scoreboard inside the computer with the command SCORE. We must tell the computer where to put the score. (I always call the scoreboard Z.) We've also got to tell the computer where to look for the result -- the Scalar J where we had stashed the result. So -- score J Z.

You said we need not just one trial "family" but a hundred families. So we've got to tell the computer to carry out this whole operation a bunch of times. We order REPEAT a hundred times to make one family. We put the REPEAT command at the beginning of the commands for a single trial, along with the number of repetitions we want, and then we use the command END to finish a repetition.

You don't need to know this word, but just for the fun of it we have just completed a "loop", which makes sense because the machine goes round and round that loop a hundred times between REPEAT and END.

When you get finished going around this loop you stop because it told you how many times to go around this loop, a hundred times. Okay? So now we've got the results of a hundred families. Right?

After we have completed our hundred families we need to check the record on our scoreboard. We COUNT among the hundred yes's (that is, 3's) and no's (that is, numbers other than 3) how many yeses there are. We put the answer in K and PRINT it.

Now we can extract our result from the machine. So we tell the machine to PRINT the result. In this case the word PRINT tells the machine to show the result on the screen. We could also print on paper. So let's actually print. [show PRINT.]

We want to know if we got three girls. See we have our scoreboard show the number of families with zero girls, one girl, two girls, three girls, or four girls, in each and every family. Of course we especially want to know how many families with three girls.

Now we must tell the computer to RUN the program. Let's.

The program is doing it, it's going through the loops right now.

Now we can look at Z for each case you looked to see the number of girls. And we can look at K to see how many families out of the hundred had three and exactly three girls.

So far we have worked problems in "probability". Let's now consider a problem in the sub-field of probability called "statistics". First I'm going to tell you something you won't believe. Professional baseball players do not suffer from slumps, and professional basketball players do not have "hot hands".

Anybody here ever hear of Larry Bird? Well, in the first three games of the 1988 NBA playoff series between Boston and Detroit, Larry Bird got only baskets 20 of the 57 shots he attempted in the first three games. Everybody agreed that Bird was in a slump. As the Washington Post said (May 30, 1988, p. D4):

Larry Bird is so cold he couldn't throw a beach ball in the ocean...

They fully expect Bird to come out of his horrendous shooting slump...

It is safe to assume that if Bird doesn't shake out of his slump Monday, it will be difficult and probably even impossible for Boston [continue]

What does "slump" mean? If it means anything it means that the chance of Bird scoring a basket at the end of that period is lower than usual. And coaches and players usually conclude that the player should take fewer shots than usual because he does not have a "hot hand".

Narrator: In a regular class, the following ideas would be drawn from the students by the instructor. For lack of time, the instructor will simply lecture.

But did Bird really have a "cool" hand? That is, was his shooting eye less good during this period than it usually is? Or could that sequence of events have occurred just by chance, just as if he was a coin, which coin cannot have a hot hand? The coin's chance of success and failure stays the same from flip to flip, even though gamblers feel that a coin or a set of dice is hot or cold when the coin shows a long run of misses. Therefore, let's see just how unusual it would be for a coin that "succeeds" 48 percent of the time to show a "slump" like Bird's.

First we generate 57 numbers between 1 and 100.

GENERATE 57 1,100 A [show on screen, or printout]

Next, we count how many of those 57 shots were "baskets", that is, were between 1 and 48 (remember that Bird is a 48 percent shooter on the average).

COUNT A between 1 48 J

Next we score the result.

SCORE J Z

Then we repeat those operations 1000 times by putting a REPEAT statement in front of those three operations that make up one trial, and an END statement after them. Our program now looks like this:

```
REPEAT 1000
GENERATE 57 1,100 A
COUNT A between 1 48 J
SCORE J Z
END
```

Afterwards, we count the number of trials in which the result is fewer than 21 baskets.

COUNT Z < 21 K

Then we PRINT the result from K, and the results for the separate trials in Z.

```
REPEAT 1000
GENERATE 57 1,100 A
COUNT A between 1 48 J
SCORE J Z
END
COUNT Z < 21 K
PRINT  Z K
```

Now let's run our program and see what we get.
[Program runs. Show program]

The results suggest that in about four trials out of a hundred, our simulated Larry Bird gets 20 or fewer baskets in 57 shots. That means that even if nothing changes in his shooting, during one in every 25 series of 57 shots, on average, he would shoot that poorly or worse. (This does not mean that the chances are 24 in 25 that such an event did not happen by chance. Rather, it means that in every hundred sets of 57 shots, we can expect four to be that poor. Similarly, we can expect some series to seem terrific when they also are occurring just by chance without a change in the system.)

It would seem, then, that it would be a mistake for the Celtics to tell Bird to do anything different after this cold streak than ordinarily. Bird should take just as many shots as usual, in his usual style, just as one continues to use a coin even after it has come down heads a bunch of times in a row. In other words, if it ain't broke, don't fix it.

Here we note the importance of the context in which we get the data. The reason we are not impressed with a 4-in-100 probability, and continue to expect that in his upcoming games Bird will have shooting success at his long-run average of 48 percent, is that Bird shoots hundreds and hundreds of shots each year, and sooner or later he will have a set of 57 shots with very poor results, a set of shots with very good results, and a variety of other outcomes. But if this were a person for whom we had no other information - say, a high school basketball player at the beginning of his first season - then our best guess would be that in the future he would shoot baskets at the rate of 20 in 57.

Understanding variability of this kind is the key to Japanese quality control, taught to them by an American statistician named Edward Deming. And resampling is a remarkably effective and easy tool to use in studying such quality control in practical situations.

APPENDIX: Table of Random Digits
(Grouped for ease of viewing)

```
48 52 78 38 11 90 41 83    43 99 51 55 57 03 83 20
15 11 84 33 09 24 08 52    42 70 37 16 66 73 15 54
25 89 70 11 91 65 41 90    88 04 30 72 15 81 34 46
34 24 66 55 67 79 29 18    36 56 96 95 35 06 05 10
37 27 58 38 23 84 94 39    99 50 74 80 41 85 98 63
12 17 04 68 19 98 53 44    16 32 91 01 71 60 19 12
88 85 44 65 52 01 99 56    72 07 96 39 56 34 86 01
81 92 77 83 10 58 92 33    63 48 62 66 32 61 59 74
08 50 15 18 13 45 65 12    32 92 53 82 07 61 71 80
84 29 90 36 05 95 20 71    17 82 83 38 01 87 74 92
77 76 46 28 47 15 04 21    04 75 51 83 91 37 14 32
01 33 90 94 86 10 03 99    95 98 76 97 97 26 45 62
49 76 58 77 29 73 99 94    83 87 61 53 47 01 15 65
54 37 39 76 71 71 36 34    47 27 98 28 95 37 67 19
67 71 32 24 49 69 55 98    89 88 15 10 27 62 28 93
07 44 34 13 52 85 68 08    28 42 54 74 05 44 04 11
54 50 82 77 72 72 24 61    73 04 81 67 62 46 80 75
27 34 87 77 94 92 63 77    93 81 86 98 11 34 56 58
49 17 80 80 34 82 97 22    71 88 20 79 76 31 31 53
06 05 70 14 19 73 13 76    29 41 93 77 35 30 48 49
93 72 31 07 47 00 68 72    29 53 10 52 23 61 84 84
20 98 01 13 96 09 91 47    42 88 78 26 90 36 46 42
55 83 54 76 79 26 62 31    83 33 68 24 73 40 48 64
19 40 71 11 86 79 02 64    85 64 49 57 07 22 81 10
43 92 26 21 00 21 54 56    20 04 37 19 68 97 34 11
17 69 22 72 81 25 31 71    92 72 28 60 49 13 66 76
69 30 08 27 97 44 48 52    15 92 46 39 18 00 50 83
19 72 87 62 41 95 37 78    10 84 44 23 83 74 32 32
37 27 27 47 09 94 57 97    90 38 37 79 59 47 42 98
77 82 56 75 10 43 33 24    74 47 75 74 76 99 14 15
33 00 01 19 52 94 65 07    18 22 44 23 06 32 21 53
32 98 20 04 66 05 69 52    67 04 34 53 87 45 17 35
52 16 14 55 21 67 66 67    50 74 58 62 04 47 78 66
85 09 39 76 53 10 52 01    52 24 81 78 30 48 43 67
20 53 91 76 36 01 37 89    08 88 06 04 13 18 97 24
30 92 02 95 78 03 71 60    54 47 10 43 95 07 06 64
46 71 96 59 09 38 41 20    86 51 71 74 16 44 85 46
28 96 35 68 36 10 43 22    56 87 60 16 97 31 53 00
50 46 09 97 14 00 24 30    97 37 82 08 00 85 05 80
65 23 10 17 07 39 29 94    12 67 52 23 85 36 04 77
94 25 40 90 95 22 46 14    34 71 70 45 97 51 68 27
69 50 64 18 30 76 47 51    02 82 30 54 22 12 35 20
12 48 72 54 97 54 82 60    18 88 55 96 90 45 77 05
23 12 27 62 74 93 44 76    68 35 21 71 11 65 65 07
34 11 27 35 35 24 83 78    12 68 18 26 75 29 15 38
48 95 67 39 84 00 17 10    10 77 22 84 48 59 97 51
56 02 95 98 91 95 11 59    34 16 22 27 57 34 92 40
36 18 42 82 36 33 09 02    59 19 59 50 57 05 80 19
13 97 78 17 46 24 07 01    83 09 22 38 09 30 89 90
48 95 57 19 34 47 99 17    05 01 99 56 84 62 72 96
09 62 89 01 53 80 89 12    73 99 95 41 48 06 05 27
82 61 87 98 29 94 03 59    58 07 05 15 92 41 26 26
12 04 44 84 02 44 50 53    53 46 40 43 38 96 83 37
05 68 19 32 55 31 79 13    09 35 26 11 23 69 41 95
```

General References

Atkinson, David T., "A Comparison of the Teaching of Statistical Inference by Monte Carlo and Analytical Methods", Ph.D. thesis, University of Illinois, 1975.

Cook, Earnshaw, Percentage Baseball, Baltimore, 1971.

Dixon, W.J., and F.J. Massey, Introduction to Statistical Analysis, 2nd ed., New York, McGraw Hill, 1957

Dunnette, Marvin D., "Fads, Fashions and Folderol in Psychology," American Psychologist XXI, April 1, 1966, pp. 343-352.

Efron, Bradley, "Computer-Intensive Methods in Statistics", Scientific American, May, 1983, pp. 116-130.

Kinsey, Alfred C., Wardell B. Pomeroy and Clyde E. Martin, Sexual Behavior in the Human Male, Philadelphia, Saunders, 1953.

Mosteller, Frederick, Robert E.K. Rourke and George B. Thomas, Jr., Probability with Statistical Applications, 2nd ed, Reading, MA, Addison Wesley, 1970.

Neyman, Jerzy, First Course in Probability and Statistics, New York, Holt, 1950.

Noreen, Eric, Computer-Intensive Methods for Testing Hypotheses, New York, Wiley, 1989.

Peterson, Ivars, "Pick a Sample," Science News, July 27, 1991, pp. 56-58.

Raiffa, Howard, Decision Analysis, Reading, MA, Addison Wesley, 1968

Schlaifer, Robert, Introduction to Statistics For Business Decisions, New York, McGraw Hill, 1959.

Science, "The Art of Learning From Experience", July 14, 1984, pp. 156-158.

Shevokas, Carolyn, "Using a Computer-Oriented Monte Carlo Approach to Teach Probability and Statistics in a Community College General Mathematics Course", Ph.D. thesis, University of Illinois, 1974.

Simon, Julian L., Basic Research Methods in Social Science, Random House, New York, 1969; second edition, 1978; third edition, with Paul Burstein, 1985; Chapters 30-34.

Simon, Julian L., and Peter Bruce, "Resampling: A Tool for Everyday Statistical Work," Chance, v. 4, no. 1, 1991, p. 22-32.

_____, and Alan Holmes, "A Really New Way to Teach Probability and Statistics", The Mathematics Teacher, Vol. LXII, April, 1969, pp. 283-288.

_____, David T. Atkinson, and Carolyn Shevokas, "Probability and Statistics: Experimental Results of a Radically Different Teaching Method", The American Mathematical Monthly, Vol. 83, November, 1976, pp. 733-739.

_____, and Dan Weidenfeld, "SIMPLE: Computer Program for Monte Carlo Statistics Teaching", American Statistician, Nov., 1974 (letter).

_____, and Derek Kumar, "SIMPLE-STATS: A Radical Teaching And Computer Program For Probability And Statistics", 1981.

Tukey, John W., Exploratory Data Analysis, Reading, MA, 1977, Addison Wesley.

Technical References

Ayer, A.J., "Chance," Scientific American, October, 1965, pp. 44-54.

J.H. Chung and D.A.S. Fraser, "Randomization Tests for a Two-Sample Problem", Journal of the American Statistical Association, 53, September, 1958, 729-35.

Meyer Dwass, "Modified Randomization Tests for Nonparametric Hypotheses", <u>Ann. Math. Statis.</u>, 29, March, 1957, 181-18.

Bradley Efron, <u>The Jackknife, the Bootstrap, and Other Resampling Plans</u>, SIAM, 1982.

R.A. Fisher, <u>The Design of Experiments</u>, Harper, 1951.

E.J.G. Pitman, "Significance Tests Which May Be Applied to Samples from Any Population", Royal Statistical Society, <u>Supplement 4</u>, 1937, 119-130.

_____, "Significance Tests Which May Be Applied to Samples from Any Population: III. The Analysis of Variance Test", <u>Biometrika</u>, 29, 322-35.

Wallis, W.A., "Some Useful Nonparametric Methods," Chicago, University of Chicago (mimeographed), October, 1957.

INDEX

RESAMPLING STATS - The "New Statistics"

Resampling - bootstrap, permutation, and other tests - has revolutionized 1990's statistics. Resampling is now the method of choice for confidence limits, hypothesis tests, and other everyday problems.

RESAMPLING STATS is an extraordinarily simple yet powerful language for the "new statistics" of resampling. Clear. Intuitive. User-friendly. No formulas or tables. Every step perfectly understood. For both experts and non-statisticians. Easy-to-read user guide, tutorial, support & consultation. For IBM & MAC: 20 years experience on mainframes & micros. Userguide available in Spanish, too. $185 ($135 academic or personal check, $79 student, $18 per disk when ordering for a class.) Video course $149. FREE 30-DAY TRIAL for software. (U.S. and Canada) (Outside North America: add $18 shipping, prepay with VISA/MC.)

● Very impressive. ... The more I work with RESAMPLING STATS, the more impressed I become. Its ease of use and computational speed are great." W. Becker, author of *Business and Economic Statistics with Computer Applications*.

● Very well designed... *Decision Line*

● Its intriguing approach sets it apart from traditional statistics packages. *Bulletin of the Ecological Society*

- -

Please send a 30-day trial copy (North America) to:

NAME: _____ Phone: _____

ADDRESS: _____

_____

Outside North America prepay with Mastercard or Visa.